When the Glitter turns to Grey

A wrestler looks back on a colourful career

Martin Gillott

MEMORIES

The audience were mesmerized, as he stood there in the ring
His long blonde hair was flowing, and his body glistening
His cloak was made of finest silk, with silver trunks and boots
Charisma flowed from every pore, Panache down to his roots

He entertained the baying crowds, with agility and speed
He dazzled us with wrestling skills, and everyone took heed
Alas now fifty years have passed, the blonde has turned to greys
And all he has, is memories, of young and glorious days

His legs are weak his back is bent, his hair went long ago
A shadow of his former self, a broken man---I know
For I was once the 'Glitterboy' with all those youthful ways
Now all that's left is photographs, of those long and far-off days

When I look into the mirror, at all that I now see
I can't believe its 'Glitterboy' that's staring back at me
If the good Lord sold us wishes, only one would I obtain
I'd turn the clock back all those years and do the same again.

Contents

Dedication 7
Acknowledgements 8
Foreword 10
INTRODUCTION 13
FAIRGROUND DAYS 16
MY FIRST TOUR 37
THE BOSTON CRAB 54
The Lady at the Back 55
MY FIRST TOUR 58
EPILOGUE 66
To Part Two 66
Early Trouble 67
Unwelcome guests 68
Sailed down the river 71
Karl Heinz 74
Alan Kilby 76
Dwight J. Ingleburgh 77
Obnoxious Fans 83
Enough is Enough 86
Working a Gimmick 87
The Beekeeper 88
The Masked Mummy 90
Another Country 91
The After-Show Party 93
Beware of What You Hear 94
The Dreaded Landladies 97

Malcolm	98
My Brother Peter	99
Injuries and Inconveniences	103
Alan Brown RIP	104
A Hair-Raising Experience	106
Memories of a Car Park	107
My Favourite Guest House	109
Not To Be Sniffed At	111
With A Little Help From My Friend	113
Championing the Cause	115
QUESTIONS I'M OFTEN ASKED	116
The Man Behind the Mask	122
Ladies of the Ring	127
Into the Woods	128
Building the Dream	130
Up On The Roof	131
Taking the Strain	132
The Garden	134
The Mixer	137
A Right Royal Muck Up	139
The Scapegoat	140
Cars That Pass in the Night	141
You Never Know	142
Tag Team	143
An Englishman, an Irishman and a Scotsman	145
Vision in Lurex	148
Pride Before A Fall	150

SENSE OF HUMOUR FAILURES	153
The Dreaded Handbag	155
FROM SPANDEX TO HANDBAGS	158
Whistle Stop Tour	160
Showered With Embarrassment	161
Late On Parade	162
The Hen Party	164
Beware of the Bikers	165
The Ride of a Lifetime	168
Holding a Grudge	170
Music to my Ears	171
Who's A Pretty Boy Then?	172
The Maverick	173
Violent Wrestlers	175
Keeping Fit	176
Hello Again Grapple Fans	179
The Day the Ring Broke Down	180
Keeping Up The Persona	182
A Change of Career	184
THE NAKED TRUTH	187
Some Sort of Idiot	188
Washday	188
The Raffle	189
Johnny Johnson	191
Treading the Boards	191
The Boys	197
A Not So Brief Encounter	200

FUNERAL OF A LEGEND	212
A Kiss Me Quick Hat and a Stick of Rock	214
North of the Border Take 2	220
I Need a Snorkel	225
Have You Got a Light Boy?	226
Menace On The Road	227
Calendar Boys	228
A Grand Day Out in Watford	230
What a Gay Day	231
The Mossblown Plaque	233
Sanjay The Promoter	236
In Your Dreams	237
A Quick Catch Up	239
Proper Celebrities	241
That's The Spirit	243
Glitterboy Goes Wild	244
Ian 'Teddy Bear' Taylor	252
Billy La Rue	253
Wrestling Heritage	255
Some Kind Words About My Last Book	256
The Mattress	257
The Flower Show	259
And Finally	264

Dedication

I dedicate this book to my wonderful granddaughter, Luna Willow Poore, to whom I once spoke the memorable words: 'If you think you are going to wrap me around your little finger, you are perfectly correct.'

Acknowledgements

First, I would like to thank all of those who have made this book possible. They include:

My lovely wife Ruth, who never complained when I took over the breakfast bar with my writings, doodles and screwed-up sheets of paper for hours on end and then spent time reading through the manuscript, dotting the 'I's 'and crossing the 'T's'.

My daughter Chloe Finlay-Black for doing such a great job of producing the artwork.

My good friend Ian 'Teddy Bear' Taylor for encouraging me to get on and finish it.

My good friend Johnny Kincaid for furnishing the much-appreciated foreword.

I would also like to thank all those wrestlers, seconds, referees and promoters who have helped me to make so many wonderful memories of my days in the ring.

Thanks also to all who purchased my first book, 'Confessions of a Wrestler'. I hope that you enjoy reading this one as much as I have writing it.

And last but in no way least, I would like to thank all those die-hard fans who would be glued to their televisions on a Saturday afternoon watching wrestling on World of Sport, many of whom would then go out, sometimes during awful weather and trudge their way to a hall nearby (or even further afield) to watch and support us all in the flesh.

Without them, we would never have been able to do what we loved doing best. I do hope that they all remember those days with the fondness that I and all my wrestling colleagues do, to this day.

Foreword
by Johnny Kincaid

I can honestly say that I never knew Martin very well back in his wrestling days. Yes, we had met a few times at various venues, and we had a few photos taken in the dressing room together, but close buddies we weren't. Many years passed, and we met up again at the funeral of Mick McManus, then again at the funeral of Peter Szakacs in Milton Keynes. After the service Martin asked if there was a local pub anywhere nearby, a nod of my head and we slipped away for a few cold beers. We sat for a few hours reminiscing about the good old days. This was the fruition of our friendship, one that has seen us travelling a lot of miles together. For instance, when we drove up to Ayr in Scotland together for a wrestler's reunion, I happened to mention that I had not booked a hotel, Martin said he had a double room booked for himself, so if I wanted, I could share with him. I said, 'That's very kind of you thank you very much'.

It was on this trip that Martin told me he had already written his own autobiography called 'Confessions of a Wrestler'. He told me his main job was as a qualified osteopath. Who said wrestlers are all brawn and no brains? We didn't talk about the wrestling – we had the whole weekend to talk about that stuff.

I'm sure if he put his mind to it, he could make a fortune on stage, because he is one hell of a funny man. When we arrived in Ayr and found the hotel, Martin went to reception, while I got the cases from the car, and when I met him in reception I asked if everything was all right about the room. I had paid for a double and now there were two of us.

When we reached the room Martin was the first through the door, and a big grin appeared on his face. There was only one bed, a double bed. Martin burst out laughing. I stood shaking my head saying 'no way, no f**king way am I sleeping in that bed with you'. He couldn't talk for laughing, and I couldn't stop repeating myself. I'd rather sleep in the car, get it changed, or try and get another room or hotel.

I thought Martin was going to collapse because he couldn't catch his breath from so much laughing. He kept pointing to the bed and when he could talk he said 'they are two singles pushed together to make a double, I'll phone reception and get them to make them up as single beds'. He started laughing again, saying 'you should have seen your face'. Don't forget that when he was wrestling, he wrestled as a gay wrestler and did a very good job of it. Now I was thinking. is he or isn't he?

Martin became a very popular figure in Scotland and the Scottish wrestlers' reunion made him their Honorary President. As all of us Englishmen know, to have any sort of title bestowed on you in Scotland, you must be something special.

I think of myself as a connoisseur of wrestlers, having been a booker for wrestlers into foreign countries, i.e. India, Lebanon, Zambia and Greece. You must know the personalities and characters of the men you are sending to represent your country as ambassadors, as well as getting along with the colleagues you are travelling with.

After spending days with Martin, I have no doubt that if his wrestling career had not come to a sharp finish, he would have made it into the ranks of superstar. It has been my pleasure and honour to write this foreword for him.

God bless my friend for life, Martin Gillott, aka Jackie Glitterboy Evans.

INTRODUCTION

Following the publishing of my first book, friends, family and quite a few old school wrestlers were enquiring when the next one was being published. It wasn't going to be easy as most of my wrestling career was covered in the first one. Luckily for me, the memories of those days have been and still are popping into my head from time to time, so I decided to get the old laptop out of the cupboard, blow the dust off and have a go.

I have agonized for a while now as to how I would proceed with this second one. As you may know, a lot of the first book was made up of a series of short stories, most of them funny things that I had come across and been involved with over my 14 + years as a wrestler, plus a short insight into how I started in the business. I have decided in this one to tell you about some of the other people that helped in some way to shape my career into what it finally became.

If you think this will be a who's who of wrestling, then you may be disappointed. I have come across many of the television wrestling stars of the day and some I will mention, but there will be many more that, unless you are in the business, so to speak, you will never have heard of. There were many good wrestlers who never did television work, but they were brilliant at what they did. It's not just me that says so, any professional wrestler worth his salt will tell you the same.

They mainly worked in the halls, fund raising fetes and even fairground booths all over the country and were the backbone of the industry for many years. Some of them were icons in the sport but had never set foot in front of a camera. These were some of the people who impressed me the most, people I wanted to emulate. Some of them (as with the well-known ones on television,) became my idols and over the years, many of them have become good friends. I make no apologies for omitting the identities of those whose names I do not wish to offend with my memories as I am not in the habit of hurting them or their loved ones for the sake of a good read. That aside, I hope that you will at least gain an insight into that wonderful time that has become known as the 'golden era of wrestling.'

I will also tell you what happened to me once I hung up my boots and launched myself into a different career. And finally, how I brought wrestling back into my life by the merest chance of going to a funeral.

Martin R. Gillott
AKA Jackie 'Glitterboy' Evans

PART ONE

FAIRGROUND DAYS

There were many ways a keen young wrestler could get into the business. Throughout the length and breadth of the UK there were wrestling gyms popping up all over the country when I started in the late 60s and early 70s, usually run by established wrestlers who wanted to pass on their skills. I myself used a gym in Birmingham known as Hadley Playing Fields, quite a large sports complex covering all kinds of different persuasions. I had been wrestling for a while when I joined this gym, but I really started like many before me and afterwards, working the boxing and wrestling booths. My nearest one belonged to a well-known showman called Ron Taylor who not only worked that area but had overwintering grounds in Gloucester.

During my time working for Ron Taylor on the boxing and wrestling booth, I managed to fight many different people from all walks of life but all with one thing in common, and that was that they all fancied themselves as wrestlers. Some, you could tell, had watched the television bouts very closely and had tried to learn from it. In fact, some had picked it up very well while others had realized that it was more difficult than they originally thought. To be honest, the majority had only been in the ring to impress their girlfriends or mates and were invariably too pissed to get up the steps into the ring let alone wrestle.

There were the odd occasions where there were no takers for the wrestling challenge, in which case we were expected to box instead. Now if you have read my previous book, you will be aware that the noble art of boxing was not my bag. There were quite a few boxing clubs around at the time but very few wrestling clubs, so it was natural that if two lads got up to box there was a fair chance that they would know what they were expected to do. If this was the case, then there was a fair chance that they would give me a right good hiding, which was not only embarrassing for me but not very endearing to the boss, who would have to pay out more of his precious money.

In one show, after taking punch after punch for two rounds from a half handy punter and without me managing to land a descent punch on him, something within me must have snapped and I found myself lifting him above my head and giving him a perfect body slam into the canvas. The crowd were going mad, and the ref didn't know whether to count him out or not. I guess he did the next best thing and disqualified me.

My opponent wasn't pleased, and neither were the ref or the crowd, and as for the boss, well, I had better pack my case now, I thought. It wasn't until the end of the night that the boss caught up with me. I think he must have been in a good mood because all he said to me was 'I hope you don't expect to be paid for that bout, and you can forget your share of the Nobbins. I had better explain what that meant for the uninitiated. The Nobbins was a whip-round from the crowd given in appreciation for the entertainment that had been provided, collected by a couple of wrestlers with an open towel so that money could be chucked in to be shared out among the booth wrestlers and boxers. On a good house, you could end up with more than you had earned from fighting. However, missing out on it was a small price to pay, I thought. Especially as I was never again asked to stand in for a boxer.

Overall, my days working the wrestling and boxing booths were great days and ones which have made many memories for me. On reflection the best times were not when I was up on the booth taking challengers but when I was in the crowd challenging the wrestlers. That was the time when I was gaining experience, learning from those who had been in the game longer than me. If you were willing to hang around as I did, you could get some feedback from the wrestler you had previously challenged. The shows were usually staged every 90 minutes so there was time to chat to the booth boys and for the price of a warm paper cup of something that masqueraded as coffee you could get valuable advice and indeed some direction personally designed to enhance your own performance that would someday improve your own game.

I must admit that at that young age, I thought I knew a fair bit about the art of wrestling. In the grand scheme of things, I quickly realized that I knew bugger all. Many wrestlers have used the fairground booths in the early days, as a stepping stone to into the business before being accepted into the realms of the independent promoters.

The main reason behind this was the fact that, although wrestling clubs and training gyms were starting up, many of them were situated in and around the larger cities and towns, and that would have meant a couple of hours' trip to their nearest one, which wasn't feasible, especially after a hard day at work, and travelling there and back two or three nights a week.

Other wrestlers would use the booths when the fairground came to town, just to keep their hand in, or to earn a little extra beer money. These wrestlers were usually experienced, but didn't relish the amount of travelling around the different venues up and down the country. I have known and worked with many great wrestlers in my time on the booths who would fit into this category. Happy to fight, providing that they can comfortably travel home to their own beds every time.

Clearly, in the past, they have had a belly full of digs, B&Bs and rabid landladies, as was the norm in those early days on the road. Speaking for myself, I enjoyed my time spent on the fairgrounds and I took full advantage of learning a lot of my trade there and from having the opportunity of working with some of the most skilful wrestlers in the business. Once you had made it to a booth boy you would then occasionally be called upon to pass on your knowledge to others who were keen to improve themselves in the ring. One thing I learned was that any wrestler at any stage of his career would always be willing to pass on his skills to others. I have gained many wrestling skills by talking to experienced wrestlers in the fairground booths.

Some of them would take you back into the ring, between shows and give you a *pull round,* a wrestling term used when they would put you through a few moves and set you right on many things that you were lacking. These sessions were always valuable to any would-be wrestler.

As time went by, I was often called upon to pass on my then limited knowledge to other wannabe wrestlers. The first thing I became aware of was the need to make sure that they were indeed genuine. Some only wanted to impress their mates or girlfriends, or as one said, he wanted to be able to give someone a good beating. Wrong answer. I wasn't interested. I will tell you about a couple of times when I found myself getting into conversations with would be wrestlers on the fairground booths. They went something like this.

<u>Candidate one – Jim (not his real name)</u>

Jim: 'Do you reckon I could get up and challenge that bloke who was up there with you? The one with the beard.'

Me: 'Oh you mean Dave, have you any experience of wrestling?'

Jim: 'I've been watching it on the television for quite a while now, and I reckon I could hold my own.'

Me: 'So you've no experience then?'

Jim: 'No, but how difficult can it be, it's just another fight and I've been in a few in my time. I'm a lot bigger than him, anyway, I have been practising my drop kick technique on a punch bag in my garage gym.'

Me: ' I think you will need a bit more than that.'

Jim: 'Why is that then?

Me: 'Because you could become dangerous to him as well as to yourself.'

Jim: (laughing) 'You mean he would be scared of losing?'

Me: 'That bloke with the beard you saw up there earlier, on the last show, is a married man with two small children, if you go in against him with your limited knowledge of the game, and cause him some serious injury, who's going to support his family if he is off work?'

Jim: 'Well, that's his problem, if I beat him in the ring, that's all fair and square.'

Me: 'Oh you won't beat him, he will dispatch you, and more than likely, you will come out of that ring and into the audience, quicker than sh*t off a shovel.'

Jim: 'I'll take my chance anyway.'

Me: ' Okay, since you seemed to have made up your mind, there really isn't anything more for me to say.'

Now the usual routine when you are in the ring with your challenger is to do the best you can for the first two rounds for the sake of giving the paying audience something for their hard-earned money, then, in the third and last round, let the beginner do his best to beat you, if he can. (By the end of the second round, you have established what is capabilities are. I was in the changing tent before the next show, and Jim had challenged Dave as he said he would. I just whispered one word in Dave's ear. I'm not going to tell you what that word was.) Dave just nodded.

The first two shows were underway with two challenging young boxers, obviously from a local club, who knew what they were doing. Both doing 3 x 3-minute rounds with the booth boxers, they held themselves well against the booth boys, both staying their distance and winning their prize money, ten bob (50p).

Then it was my turn in the ring. My opponent was one who had challenged me several times that fortnight, and although not that experienced, he was keen to learn and held himself well. I had taken him in the ring for a pull round a couple of times before and he had taken on board a few pointers that I had given him. It turned out to be a good bout.

Then it was Dave's turn, again, the usual 3 x 3-minute rounds. The bell rang out for round one as they came together in the middle of the ring. A few headlocks and armlocks later and Dave threw his opponent against the ropes. Jim came off the ropes, raised one leg in the air, pulled his knee towards him and kicked Dave in the chest with full force. Dave toppled but stayed on his feet. The bout, from then, got very sloppy until Dave threw him, once more, on to the ropes. He came off the ropes again with one leg in the air for his famous drop kick. Dave sidestepped him, grabbed his raised foot and kicked his other leg from under him. He went down onto the canvas with such a bang, the whole ring shook, and his leg was doubled up underneath him. The ref stopped the bout. He didn't even attempt to start the count of ten, the screams and yells must have been heard all over the fairground as the first aider climbed into the ring. He took one look at him and went off to call an ambulance.

A while later when the crowd had left, he was transported to the hospital, still screaming in pain. I had no idea what he had done, but I reckon he must have spent several weeks in a plaster cast at the very least. Poor bugger, out in the first round and he never even got to spit in the bucket.

That is what can happen when you're attitude is all wrong. I did tell him, but he clearly thought that his way was the best.

Candidate two, Mark (name changed)

This young lad turned out to be quite different from the last one. He was mad keen on the wrestling game and had a good attitude towards it. I had seen him many times at various places where there happened to be a fairground with our wrestling booth. I had also been challenged by him a few times as well as other wrestlers, keen to amass as much knowledge and experience as he could get.

He had also obtained the boots, leotard etc, which apparently his parents had bought him for his birthday and Christmas presents. Here was a lad who took his wrestling seriously and I had high hopes for his future.

Two weeks after I had left the fairground life, to work for the independent promotions, I heard the news that Ronnie Taylor had taken him on as a booth boy. I was so pleased for him.

About four years later I was on the bill in Taunton. I had wrestled that venue a few times, but I didn't recognize the name of my opponent. Imagine my surprise and delight when I found he was this young lad from the booths. He had, of course, changed his name and was as surprised as me, because I had also changed mine, to Jackie 'Glitterboy' Evans.

My first impressions were that in the last four years, he had become a great wrestler and, that night, he certainly made me work for my corn. We had a drink after the show and he told me that he had spent a total of three seasons with Ronnie, working the booths before moving on to the independent circuit. We finally said our goodbyes and yes, I was on the same bill and wrestled him many times after that. Forty-plus years later, we still meet up at some of the reunions and raise a drink to those far-off days and the magic that the fairgrounds brought to our lives. Regardless of your status in the wrestling world, good, sound advice was always available. I will tell you now of some of those wrestlers who have been of great help to me in my early years. It was thanks to those guys and to the hours I put in the gym and a wrestling club in Birmingham that I was able to reach my goal.

Johnny Diamond

I first met Johnny Diamond in the late 60s or early 70s on the fairground booth in Gloucester. Johnny, real name Johnny Emms, used the name Diamond because he was a very accomplished jeweller. From Birmingham, he was a small whippet of a wrestler and as fast as they come in the ring. Like many, he was skilful and would readily pass on these skills to others. He would turn out to be my main mentor in the early days.

Having been fortunate to train on a Sunday morning at Hadley Playing Fields gym in Birmingham, I was delighted to find that this was his training ground also and along with another great wrestler, Reg Yates, they were responsible for the success of my whole wrestling career. To those two, I remain eternally grateful.

In fact, Johnny was to teach me what would become the most valuable lesson I would ever learn. It was the first time that I had faced him as an opponent. All that camaraderie that I had experienced with him during training had been put to one side and I can honestly say that by the end of that bout, I had earned my money. He never gave an inch. Every move that I managed to put on him I had to work hard for it.

Of course, that was how it should be, and I wouldn't have had it any different. I did manage to last 5 rounds before he had the second pinfall over me, and I had been thoroughly thrashed. I, of course had no chance to get a pinfall on him, I could never hang on to him long enough for that. I had been totally outwrestled by a better man. I wasn't downhearted – how could I be? I had learned a valuable lesson.

The following Sunday morning at the gym went the same as usual and he put me through my paces whilst the bout we had had a couple of nights earlier was never again mentioned. Yes, I will always be grateful (not to mention respectful) to the great Johnny Diamond and yes, as his wrestling name indicated, he was indeed a jewel among men.

I had the good fortune to meet him in the ring quite a few times, but it will always be that first bout we had together that will stay in my memory.

Pat 'Bomber' Roach

There's very little that I can say about Pat that hasn't been said already. I first met him one Sunday morning whilst training in Birmingham in the early 70s. I wouldn't say that he was a regular there as he had his own gym in the area, but we were given the pleasure of his company occasionally, and a real pleasure it was. In his early days he was billed as Irish Pat Roach and then Pat Roach and finally he wrestled as Pat 'Bomber' Roach, having met with great success playing the key role in that wonderful television series *Auf Wiedersehen Pet* as the gentle giant from Bristol, 'Bomber Brian Busbridge.'

Pat will always be thought of in wrestling circles as the man who kept us young ones on the straight and narrow. If he said something, then you listened. A massive ambassador to the wrestling world, Pat would take no nonsense from us youngsters.

I remember one young wrestler who refused to sign an autograph for a budding fan. He was immediately leapt on by Pat, who said.' Never forget boy, it's people like him that make it possible for people like you to do what you love doing, so get out there and thank him for his support and give him your bloody autograph and don't let me have to say that to you again.' A great man who was a great wrestler, who became a great friend, and is sadly missed by all who knew him.

Killer Ken Davies

Killer Ken Davies was a wrestler whose career in the ring was mainly limited to the 60s and the 70s. Billed from Tredegar, Killer Ken Davies was the long-time Welsh welterweight champion. He beat Ken Else in 1962 for the Independent Promoters British Welterweight title. Ken was a hard man from a coal mining background, but despite being a fantastic and well thought of wrestler, he was never attracted by the bigger promotions.

Many times nowadays when I am in the company of former wrestling colleagues and ask them if they had ever fought Killer Ken Davies, it surprises me how many have over the years. If one says to me that he can't remember, then I usually say to them 'you obviously haven't, otherwise you would have remembered.' I certainly did.

I first met Ken Davies early on in my career. It was a particularly wet and miserable day as we both stood up there on the fairground-wrestling booth of Mr Ron Taylor. If my memory serves me correctly, it was my fourth day on the booth and not only was I green as to the workings of such a game but my wrestling skills at that time were very much wanting.

There were also a couple of local boxers on the front as it was the norm to have two bouts of boxing followed by two bouts of wrestling. Due to the weather on that evening, the audience was thin on the ground. Luckily, with the expert help of Ron on the microphone, we were able to find a couple of local lads who were willing to take on the two boxers, but even with the banter from the owner, he was unable to find a couple of budding wrestlers willing to have a go.

'There's only one thing to do lads,' he said. 'You'll have to fight each other.' That's fine by me I thought, it's a fight and a payday and what's more, I may gain a bit more experience if this Ken bloke's a good one. We went to the changing tent, where we waited for the audience to pay and take their places in the tent.

I had noticed that my opponent was a very well-spoken and no doubt well educated man and that we were both of roughly the same height and build. *I'm going to enjoy this,* I thought as we entered the ring. The introductions were made to the audience, and the bell rang out for the first round.

From that moment on, life became very difficult. He grabbed me by the head and threw me the full length of the ring. I sat there with my legs outside the ring with the bottom rope digging into my chest. I don't know how I did it, but I was up by the count of seven and walked straight into a forearm smash which sent me flying back to where I had just come from. Bloody hell, I thought. If he throws me any harder, I'm going to end up sat on the bloody dodgems next door.

I staggered back to my feet, only to end up face down in the audience. It was at this moment that I thought to myself that the only way to stop him was to hit back and hit back hard. I got back in with the help of the audience and managed to get him in a headlock. That's it, I thought, I'll just hang on for dear life until the bell goes, but Ken had other ideas. He picked me up to head height and dropped me straight onto the canvas. I got up again to meet another flurry of forearm smashes, each one placed accurately on my chin, until the bell rang out loud for the end of round one. Round two was no better and by the middle of round three, I just wanted to die.

Through what can only be seen as divine intervention I managed to last the three twenty-minute rounds, as it seemed, rather than three minutes, and exited the ring. How I managed to get back to the changing tent I still do not know.

Killer Ken came up to me and his opening words were 'Are you going to continue to wrestle?' 'Indeed, I am' I said. 'I want to congratulate you. I'm impressed' he replied.

I looked at him and smiled. 'Thank you, was I okay?'

'No. You were bloody rubbish, but if you are willing to continue after what I did to you, it impresses me. Many would-be wrestlers don't. I wish you all the best for the future.'

I came up against Ken quite a few times after that and having got to know him, I have to say two things about this man. First, he was a complete gentleman and second, he was the hardest wrestler I ever encountered in my whole career.

I emphasize 'hardest', but that doesn't mean he was dangerous. Far from it, believe me, I knew danger getting in the ring with all those drunken guys fresh from the pub. It was just that every time you fought him you would end up with more rope and mat burns than was normal. Usually, these burns lasted a day or two. The ones he gave lasted a week or more.

These are just a few of the most interesting wrestlers that I have met and indeed have had an influence on my wrestling career. We will meet many more as this book progresses.

Independent Promotions

Having left the fairground life behind me, the next natural progression in my career was to work for the many independent wrestling promotions dotted throughout the United Kingdom. There were a few that didn't take on youngsters at all, a few that would only want you at the last minute and expected you to drop everything and run to their call, and those that wanted you to travel miles and miles for a pittance, but luckily, the majority were willing to give you a fair trial to see if you could do the business. To name but a few, There was Orig Williams, Evan Trehearne, (who also produced the *Ringsport* wrestling magazine), Associated Promotions from Bristol and in the south there was Ian Dowland from Portsmouth, Gordon Corbett and Brian Dixon. The list goes on.

Many wrestlers of the day that would do a bit of promoting from time to time, me included. But I soon decided which side of the ropes I would rather be. Thank goodness for those die-hard promoters who would allow me the chance to step into that square circle and do what I loved doing best.

'Jumping' Jim Moser

Those Promoters who were willing to use you on their shows were responsible for me making the acquaintance of many more wrestlers, each one a character. The first one that springs to mind worked under the name of Jumping Jim Moser, a gentleman of Asian extraction who was well known among promoters. When I call him a gentleman that is exactly what I mean. I introduced myself when we first met by saying, 'Hi Jim, I'm the Glitterboy and am pleased to meet you.'

He stood up and offered me his hand, which I duly shook. 'My dear boy' he said in a manner that would have made Lord Bertie Wooster proud. 'It's jolly nice to meet you, I understand we are on together tonight, I hope you will be gentle with me.' He was joking about that last statement of course. What gave it away was the fact that I had never seen such muscles on an upper body as I saw on this chap. Oh god, here comes another good hiding.

I could not have been more wrong. He was in my terms a dream to wrestle with.

Don't get me wrong – he had the upper hand all the time, there was no doubt about that, but when he had hold of you, he used just enough pressure to keep you there and you needed all your skills to get out of it. A great exponent of the drop kick, in which he would use enough pressure to take you off your feet, not like some, who would kick you into next week. He was the expert in that move, and I think that's where he got the name 'Jumping' Jim Moser.

Right through the bout he made me reach deep down for any skills that I had to keep the fight alive, me using everything and him using just enough. I knew he could have tied me up in knots had he so wished, but he didn't. He reminded me of a cat that jumps from one wall to another and just makes it – however short the distance the cat uses no more energy that it takes to complete the distance, even though it could leap three times as far. Jim passed away a couple of years ago, but he will live on in my memory.

Quite a few wrestlers would also turn their hand at promoting. Some of them would do a bit now and again, and others would make it as full-time promoters. I have even had a bash at it a couple of times myself. It wasn't for me though, and I soon stopped. A lot of first-time promoters would start off doing local fetes and private functions. One such function comes to mind – I confess that I have forgotten who the promoter was, but I will tell the story all the same.

The Hippy Bout

It was in the early days of my career when I was asked to fight in that grand old city of Bath. Not in the City Hall or anything of great architectural grandeur but in a nearby field. We were the main attraction at what can only be described as a hippy convention. I'd never actually heard of one before, so I didn't know what to expect.

The bit that caused me concern was that I was under the impression that all hippies stood for peace and harmony, so what were they going to think when two blokes got up and started to hit the hell out of each other? I guessed the promoter knew what he was doing, so I managed to put it to the back of my mind.

The day arrived and I made my way to Bath. Easy enough to find with the aid of a good map, but locating the right field was a nightmare. After several miles of driving and enquiring at several places, I managed to find it. I parked the car and having tripped over several tent guy ropes and nearly stood on a guitar left outside a tent, I found myself at the ringside.

'Where are the changing rooms?' I asked,

'In that tent there' came the reply.

'What, a whole tent to myself?'

'No, that's for all of you.'

A two-berth tent for eight wrestlers and a ref?' I thought. 'That's going to be interesting.

'I don't suppose there's any chance of getting a shower?'

He looked sideways at me. I looked around at the state of some of the crowd. 'I thought not' I said. I wasn't sure that any of them had heard of a shower.

Other wrestlers were starting to arrive and judging by the bewilderment on their faces they hadn't wrestled at one of these before either. 'Better wait for Tony' said one. 'He's behind the booking of this one.'

We spent a relaxing ten minutes waiting for him to arrive whilst listening to the tunes of one hippy strumming out his version of *Jennifer Juniper* on his guitar and singing along. Not bad, I thought, considering he only had three strings on the damn thing. He was hampered even further by the fact that he only knew one song. If I never hear that song again it will be too soon.

Eventually we got underway. I was first in the ring, having spent the previous fifteen minutes trying to get my wrestling gear on in such a confined space with tights twisted and boots on the wrong feet. As soon as I was introduced by the MC I started to strut my stuff. Mincing around the ring with full make-up on my face, sequins on my cheeks, glitter everywhere, my brightly sequinned gown flowing behind me, I looked around the audience. Now normally this spectacle would incite a lot of jeering, booing and general ridicule from the onlooking public. This time, nothing. Not even a titter. I looked around and saw the reason why. Half the audience were dressed the same - loud colours, sequins, make-up. The whole nine yards. This is going well, I thought.

I grabbed my opponent's arm and threw him into the corner post. I've got to make the crowd hate me, I thought. Nope! It wasn't happening. It was complete silence except for one bloke that stood up and shouted, 'Hey man, don't do that, you'll hurt him, peace man, be kind to him man.' I couldn't believe it; he even got a round of applause.

That bout only lasted three rounds before we'd given up the ghost and quite possibly the will to live. The ref, God bless him, disqualified me without even a public warning for upsetting the crowd. One of them stood up and started crying because I had head-butted my opponent.

'Don't do that man,' he cried 'You'll cause brain damage.' That's it, I thought. Something finally snapped inside my head and I shouted back, 'You're a fine one to talk, slurring your words. With that s**t you've been smoking I don't think you should lecture me on brain damage.' He started to cry, so three of his mates sat him down, patted him a bit and started to sing him a gentle lullaby to calm the bad vibes.

The upshot of it was that the four bouts were reduced to two by mutual consent of the promoter and the management and the show was put down as a bad idea all round. I have been instrumental in helping take down the ring many times but that one was dismantled in record time, put on the lorry and away as quick as possible Many wrestlers will talk about the highlights of their careers. This wasn't one of mine. In fact, I felt as if I had hit rock bottom.

Pedro the Gypsy

Nowadays as I sit at home with my slippers and cocoa and think back to my ring days, I must admit that some memories tend to get a bit hazy, and I regret to say that many memories have escaped me forever. Sadly, this is not to my advantage, especially when you are searching what little brain you have left for suitable material for another book. Talking to other wrestlers about the good old days, I am reminded about things that happened all those years ago. This is one of those tales. It was the first time I came across a well-known wrestler of the day called Pedro the Gypsy.

Let me tell you about it. It took place somewhere in the Midlands. I don't remember the venue, but the bout was relayed to me by a wrestler who had appeared on the same bill and who clearly had a better memory than me. I had arrived early and was enjoying a nice cup of tea when a wrestler friend of mine, Klondyke Jake, gave me a bit of advice.

'Are you on with Pedro?' he asked.

'Yes' I replied. 'I've never worked with him before, what's he like?'

Jake smiled. 'He's a prince among men' he replied with a wry smile on his face. 'I'll just give you one piece of advice. Before you go into the ring, just loosen the strings on your trunks a bit.'

'What for?' I replied.

'Just do it!' he shouted over his shoulder as he left the changing room. Mmm, I thought. I put it down to some joke that I wasn't privy too and thought no more about it. It was a while later in the second round of our bout when the wise words of Jake came home to roost. I had already surmised that Pedro's forte seemed to be taking the rise out of his opponent in, shall we say, an amusing way, or to be more precise, whatever you tried to do to him he would somehow turn the tables at the last moment and make you look a right plonker. Nothing offensive mind, just enough to entertain the crowd. He was a great wrestler giving a first-class performance to please the crowd.

I threw him against the ropes and headbutted him in the stomach. After absorbing this punishment a few times, he came off the ropes and leapt over me, coming down behind me and grabbing my trunks on the way. His idea was to expose my arse to the crowd. All the advice I had been given by Jake earlier was beginning to make sense as I heard a great ripping of the strings around my middle and saw the trunks drop around my ankles. I rushed to pull them up, but there was nothing to hold them in place. He really went to town then, throw after throw, only allowing me enough time to pull them up then down, they came again and so on and on it went until he put me out of my misery and got a pin fall over me, though what that must have been like from the front row I can only imagine. The crowd was going wild at this impromptu lesson of anatomy at my expense.

I felt embarrassed to say the least as I left the ring in record time, only to be greeted by Jake and his well-deserved 'I told you so'. I rushed to leave the hall and get back to the safety of my digs. That didn't work well either, as the lady of the house, who came home later, was sitting in the second row back and relayed the story to everyone in the place on her return. I decided not to stay for breakfast the following morning.

MY FIRST TOUR

I had only been working for the independent promoters for a few weeks after leaving the fairground booth when a phone call came in asking me if I was interested in a 12-day tour of the West Country. Of course I leapt at it; I hadn't expected to be offered this so early in my career.

We were all invited to meet up in a pub in Gloucester to be told the details and to meet the promoter. The meeting was set for Thursday night at 7.30pm, three days away. As I said it was early in my career, so wrestling work was not so plentiful. I looked forward to the challenge – it might well be my first step on a very long ladder.

I arrived on time and met up with a wrestler called Alex who was a fair bit older than me – I knew him from the fairground booth. He knew a fair bit about the game and had met a lot of promoters. 'Have you met this Alistair bloke who's promoting this tour?' I asked. 'I've never met him, but I've heard about him.' he replied.

My next question was the obvious one. 'Is he okay for the wages?'

'He always pays on time but it's never top dollar, just think of it as an experience.'

'What else have you heard about him? I asked.

'He's a bit of a spiv and from Romany stock, worth a few bob, lives in a big house in Brockworth, drives a flash car, been promoting about a year now, mainly tours like this one.'

The next to arrive introduced himself as Alex from Bath and reminded me of an Oxford student. He talked very posh and dressed well. I have been in the wrestling game long enough to know that wrestlers come in all shapes and sizes. Alex told us that he took up wrestling just to annoy his father, who was a barrister and was very disappointed in his son because he hadn't followed in daddy's footsteps.

Shortly after, Andy and his mate Richie, who both lived in Bath, arrived. They admitted that they were both inexperienced, but if they fought each other they could put on a decent show. They had learned the basics in a small club in Bath, but that was all the training that they had done. It was becoming apparent to me that this whole thing was beginning to look a bit dodgy and might not turn out as I had expected.

Finally, two more arrived. One of them was an occasional wrestler that I also remembered from the booth. He would turn up a few times when it suited him and as I remember, he was a miserable bugger, glass half empty sort of bloke, by the name of Roger, or Rog, as he preferred to be called.

The other chap introduced himself as Alistair the promoter and yes, he did seem to be a bit of a spiv. Roger piped up, 'If you find the name Alistair a bit of a mouthful, just call him Reeky. You'll know why when you've travelled with him for a few miles in a hot car.' The promoter took no notice of what I thought was an insult. Clearly there was no love lost between them, but it was apparent that they had history between them.

We all chatted small talk for a while then Reeky laid out a plan of action. Our venues for the tour were Gloucester, Swindon, Trowbridge, Salisbury, Bournemouth, Weymouth, Exeter, Exmouth, Plymouth, Truro, Barnstaple and finally Taunton. We were not expected to drive (which seemed a bonus) – a minibus had been hired and bed & breakfast was provided. Our first venue was in Gloucester and by arrangement with the pub management, we could leave our vehicles here. The ring and the ring riggers would be travelling ahead of us to set-up for each show and would double up as referee and timekeeper, Reeky would be the Master of Ceremonies. We would be paid after each show. The money wasn't great and whilst he had paid for digs and travel, I soon realized that he oversaw expenses (a shrewd man indeed). The show would consist of Andy and Richie for the opening bout and the rest of us would compete in a knockout tournament for the West Country Wrestling Cup. Two bouts, and the winners of those would compete in the final. Sounds simple enough, I thought, but miserable Roger had doubts and a lot of questions. (better get more beers in lads).

Q. Who gets top billing then?

A. well there's not really a top billing as it's a knockout situation. Fair enough I thought.

Q. when do we start? A. This Saturday.

Q. I take it that the posters are already out then? I only ask because none of us have agreed to do it yet.

A. Ah yes that is a fair point, however you will all have different names for that very reason.

Okay, so now it began to look very dodgy. He read out our new names. I can't remember the others, but I had landed the name of 'Skip Holland'. Who the bloody hell was Skip Holland? Did he ever exist? No of course he didn't.

'Hey lads, you've got work, you're earning money, what is the problem?' said Reeky. Alex spoke up: 'It's a bloody cake and arse party.' A saying he had, and I was sure it wouldn't be the last time we would hear it.

The meeting finished and we all decided that we needed another drink. Reeky took his leave and arranged that we would all meet up at six on Saturday night and drive the short distance on the other side of Gloucester to the venue in the minibus. We stayed talking for about an hour, not knowing if we should celebrate or start crying into our beer, no doubt time would tell. We eventually said our goodbyes and went our separate ways.

At the agreed time and day, we were all waiting in the car park for Reeky to appear. It was 6.15pm when the minibus pulled into the car park. We took one look at it and our jaws dropped. It was the roughest, rustiest old banger I had ever seen outside a scrapyard. I must admit that the engine sounded great, as it practically purred around the car park, but the rest of it was awful.

Reeky turned off the engine and leapt out and said, 'all aboard the Skylark'.

'Don't you mean albatross?' said posh Keith.

'I know it's appearing a bit tatty in places, but you'll be okay' said Reeky.

It was Andy that spoke next as we boarded. 'Tatty? look at it, there's more stuffing come out of the upholstery than left in it, can we put our cases in the storage bins?'

'Er, no' said Reeky, 'it hasn't got a floor to it. Stick yours on the back seats next to mine.' We were not a happy bunch. The thought of travelling all those miles over the next ten days filled me with dread.

'What's in this box?' asked miserable Roger.

'Oh, that's the West Country Cup,' said Reeky.

Roger undid the box and lifted it out. 'West Country Cup? then why has it got Colebrook Ladies Bowls Club etched into it?'

Reeky was quick to reply. ' Oh yes, that reminds me, if you have to have any photos taken with it remember to hold the etched side into your body.'

We all looked at each other, 'I don't suppose you know which of us wins it?' said Alex.

'Well you can take it in turns over the next ten days,' Reeky replied. 'Mind you, I will have to get it back at the end, I've only borrowed it.'

Alex shook his head. 'Cake and arse, absolute cake and arse.'

After a short drive, we arrived at a place called the Wooton Hall Club. 'Not exactly the Royal Albert Hall is it?' muttered Andy as we stood outside. 'Where's Reeky?'

Richie spoke. 'Parking the dustbin around the back, I guess it doesn't do for wrestlers to be seen arriving in that piece of s**t.'

We entered the hall which, as we were early, was empty except for the bar staff who were getting ready for the crowd to arrive I had to look twice but yes, there was no doubt about it, the last time I saw that ring it was in Ronnie Taylor's booth. 'Does he know that you have borrowed it?' I said as Reeky entered the hall. 'I haven't borrowed it, I've hired it, he's back in Gloucester overwintering, he won't need it for a few months.'

I took a deep breath as I wondered what other surprises we still had to come.

The first bout went well, and the two young lads put on a good show and warmed up the crowd for the main events.

Alex and I were on next. After the interval it was the turn of Keith and Roger, and finally it was the turn of the two winners who were Keith and Alex. After eight rounds, the winner was Keith. The cup was presented by none other than... the caretaker of the hall. Never mind, the crowd thoroughly enjoyed the show.

A drink at the bar and a few autographs later we were back on board the albatross and the cup was safely in the box. We were looking forward to a Chinese meal, then on to our digs in Cirencester for a good night's sleep. The nearest Chinese was a takeaway only, so we had to eat it on our way, not the easiest meal to eat on a bumpy road but just one more hurdle to get over. Let's hope our digs are okay.

As it turned out, the B&B was mediocre, but that was slightly better than we were expecting. The bed was small but comfortable. The breakfast was also small but comfortable and cooked by the elderly owners and it tasted good, even though the wait was about an hour and then they came out one plate at a time with a five-minute wait between plates.

Eventually we were ready to leave for our next destination. The busy town of Swindon surely would have a decent-sized town hall at least. However, it wasn't Swindon itself, we were fighting in the Wootton Bassett Memorial Hall, which turned out to be a lot smaller. Oh well, another day, another dollar, at least we would be able to settle into our digs before the match, maybe have a sleep for a while.

'Before you settle into your digs you might want to get a meal inside you' said Reeky as he pulled into a transport café. A pleasant hour and a big greasy all-day breakfast (the second that day) inside us and we were ready for anything, at least that's what we thought. We drove out of Wootton Bassett into what we assumed was the countryside, up a long hill and turned into a field opposite a large airfield. There in the corner of this large field was a bloody caravan. It must have been related to our minibus because it had a similar dress code. The following words came from various mouths: 'A bloody caravan,' 'you must be joking,' No expense spent here then,' 'Goodness me, whatever next? (Posh Keith.) And yes, you've guessed it, 'Cake and arse party.' (Alex.)

I must say that was the worst digs by far. Most of us were moaning about it and those that didn't were stuck for words. Reeky, who never hung about, said that he would be back for us at 6 pm and in the meantime 'make yourselves at home gents'. Surprisingly we all managed to get our sleeping arrangements sorted, as there was more room inside than it looked from outside. I reckon it was once owned by Doctor Who.

6 pm couldn't come quick enough. Reeky came for us bang on time, but none of us had anything to say to him or to each other. We were alone with our own thoughts and my thoughts were how many more bad surprises are we going to get? After all, this was only the second day. Mind you, I can't vouch for the thoughts of others.

When we finally arrived at the hall, it reminded me of the Dad's Army Church Hall in Walmington-on-Sea, maybe a bit bigger. The changing room was a small room behind the stage and we all crammed in side by side. I can't describe how small it was but I'm sure that I had someone else's leg in my tights at one time.

The caretaker knocked on the door and popped his head round to ask if there was anything we needed. 'Any chance of getting a cup of tea or coffee mate?' I asked. He replied, 'I'll see what I can do' and disappeared. He came back with an electric kettle full of water, milk, cups, spoons, sugar, tea and coffee.

'Thank you' I said, 'you are the hero of the day.' He smiled a big toothless grin and left. I never thought the day would come when the biggest victory over two days was to get a cup of tea. I felt like Steve McQueen in The Great Escape.

The wrestling match started well to a packed audience, which wasn't difficult as the size of the hall meant that four or five big families would have filled it. Miserable Roger won it that night and the cup went straight back into the box at the end of the show. We were in the changing room packing up when Posh Keith came in. 'Have you seen the posters? No? they are all the same with a space left at the top to put in the venue, date and where to buy tickets, put in with a felt tipped pen, no expense paid.' We all said in unison, 'cake and arse party'.

When we got back to our caravan, a few of us stood outside looking at the airfield over yonder and seeing all the twinkling lights. 'Do you reckon they are waiting for a plane?' said one. 'Let's hope it's our bloody Red Cross parcels,' said another. We all eventually turned in tired, cold, uncomfortable and bloody annoyed.

Day three started as we boarded the albatross on our way to our next venue in Trowbridge with a unanimous threat from us all that if we didn't stop for breakfast within the next thirty minutes, we would castrate the driver. He said nothing and within twenty minutes we were tucking into a hearty breakfast. Back on board, we were on our way to Trowbridge. We would be there in about an hour, just in time for dinner.

What a pleasing site the Town Hall was, spacious and with all the facilities we could possibly need. A grand entrance hall with a lovely staircase up to the function room. We checked out the changing rooms, perfect in every way. 'Don't get carried away,' said Posh Keith, 'we have to check out the digs first'. We were once more deflated as we left to see the digs.

'Ah well' said Andy as we reached our destination, which was on a farm, again out in the countryside. 'We certainly get a variety in this job if nothing else, who's sleeping with the pigs?

'Don't tempt fate!' shouted miserable Roger.

We were shown to our 'rooms' by the farmer's wife. In an empty enclosed barn, old hospital beds were laid out along two walls with bales of hay laid out three high dividing the bed spaces. A small cupboard with towels and soap in with a bowl stood on the top for each person. 'The toilet is on the end through that little door there and someone will bring hot water for you in the morning,' said our host. 'Breakfast from 8 am until 9 in the farmhouse. Oh and by the way, we bring Bernard the donkey in here out of the cold at night, he won't be no trouble.'

'A donkey?' said Posh Keith as our host had left us. 'Well that will make seven donkeys all told.'

Alex spoke up. 'I'll tell you now, if three wise men turn up, I'm f***ing off.' We all started to laugh out loud, I don't know if it was humour or hysteria. It was early afternoon when the farmer's wife took pity on us and invited us into the farmhouse for a cup of tea and a piece of cake. This welcome treat turned out to be tea, toast, homemade cake and biscuits followed by apple pie and cream. Then back to the barn for a quick nap.

The show that evening appeared to be the best yet with me winning the cup, a quick drink at the bar and back to the barn for what turned out to be the best night's sleep so far. Next day an all you can eat farmhouse breakfast. We were all so contented with the hospitality that we had been shown that we had a whip round for our hosts.

Our next port of call was Salisbury. 'Where are we sleeping tonight? in tents on Salisbury Plain?' said miserable Roger. He got no answer from Reeky, who was pretending to be concentrating on his driving. It wasn't a long journey, and we stopped on the way at a roadside café for an early lunch. We couldn't get into the hall until 4 pm and check in at the digs was 2 pm. We spent a good hour and a half over lunch, in fact I ate so much that with the big breakfast earlier, I thought I might have trouble getting into the ring.

I can't remember where the place was, but it was a few miles outside the city centre. When we arrived it looked a decent sized hall from the outside, but we were far too early to get in, so we went to find our digs. A mediocre sort of place, not the best but not the worst. Reeky had dropped us off and went to see how the tickets were selling.

We settled into our rooms then went down to the television/games room until he picked us up at 6 pm as usual. Apparently, the tickets had not gone too well and it was only just over half full. It turned out to be a nice hall with adequate facilities and by the time the crowd came in, more tickets were sold on the door, so the hall ended up three quarters full, not a bad house.

Talking among ourselves we had a feeling he was going to ask us to take a cut in wages, but he didn't – he probably thought he had upset us quite enough for one tour. The audience seemed very quiet at the beginning and the two young lads had their work cut out warming them up, but we all got through it, and I reckoned that by the end of the evening they had enjoyed themselves and judging by the feedback afterwards they felt that they had got their money's worth, what more can you ask?

Afterwards, back at our digs, we relaxed over a nice cup of tea and retired to our beds. The next day we were off to Bournemouth. I had been there a couple of times before but that was in the summer; I had yet to see it out of season. We were informed on our journey that we were off to a place about four miles inland but still in the Bournemouth area. I don't remember the name of the place, but the hall was long and thin, and once the ring was up, there was only room for one row of chairs each side but about twenty rows front and back. The other drawback was a low false ceiling with two-foot square ceiling tiles set in an aluminium frame, so by the time we stood in the ring, we could touch the ceiling.

It was early so we left the hall and went in search of our digs. Again they were okay, but the furniture could have been made during the war years. I think it was called utility furniture, designed simply but functional. It worked okay but if you were around it for too long it was depressing. We all decided to have a drink in a nearby pub and perhaps get a bar meal then back to the digs to be picked up. It was to no avail as the pub didn't open until six, so it was a snack and a cuppa at a twee tea shop with tablecloths and waitresses in pinafore aprons and mob caps, not really our style but welcome all the same even though we felt and probably looked out of place.

We did, however, have a laugh with the waitresses, Jenny and Maureen, nothing bawdy, just a bit of light banter. Eventually we said our goodbyes and wandered back to the digs, when it was nearly time to board the albatross and away to the venue. We were able to get tea and coffee at the venue and still had an hour to kill before the show started, so we relaxed for a while with some of us playing cards whilst a couple of us read the paper and attempted the crossword puzzle.

Richie, who had been out to check the crowd that were now arriving, came back in. 'Guess who's just come in, Jenny and Maureen, the two waitresses from the café, sitting down the side near the red corner. We'll get them going tonight.' Richie and Andy were first on as usual and ended the bout with a draw, one pinfall each and left the ring to great applause.

By then the waitresses were left in no doubt what we were doing there. We had not mentioned it earlier, so I guess it was quite a surprise for them. We had noticed that the two young lads had improved their game over the few days that we had known them. It was the consensus that they should no longer be joined at the hip and share the ring with the rest of us. We decided to leave it for now and have a word with Reeky.

The wrestling went well except that by the time it was finished, most of the ceiling tiles above the ring had been kicked out of alignment. The ring riggers replaced them with no damage caused, so everyone was happy. Well, except the booking clerk, who insisted that they get a fee of 10% for selling the tickets. Reeky didn't go much on this idea, especially as he had taken the money for the walk-ins on the door himself.

Jenny and Maureen had stayed behind and suggested that we get a couple of taxis back to the pub opposite our digs for a drink or two. 'We can get a lock in there,' said Jenny. Alex and Roger declined and went back to the digs with Reeky, and the four of us plus the two girls went to the pub.

True enough, we had a lock-in. Needless to say that there were many questions about the world of wrestling to be answered, but nothing that we had not been asked many times before. 'Is it fixed?' Posh Keith rolled up his trouser leg and displayed some rather nasty scars on his leg. 'That's where an 18 stone wrestler tried to bite a chunk out of my leg.'

'Oh my god!' said Maureen, 'I'll never think of wrestling in the same way again.'

'How did you get those scars?' I whispered to Keith. 'Fell off my bike when I was a kid' came the reply.

The young barmaid came out with a plate of sandwiches in one hand and a plate of cake in the other. Keith and I noticed how short her mini skirt was. When she put the plates down on a low table, Posh Keith said, 'now that's what I call a cake and arse party.' I spurted my drink everywhere. Just before midnight we took our leave after thanking them for their hospitality. It was a cold night, there was a breeze blowing, and the stars were shining bright as we headed back to our digs to face the wartime furniture. 'Ah well' said Posh Keith, 'let's get in before the bombs start dropping.'

The following day saw us travelling to Weymouth, just along the coast. We relayed our previous night's antics to those who didn't attend. 'Hey Reeky, where do you bugger off to when you drop us off?' said Richie. 'Oh, here and there, always things to do,' he replied. 'And where do you sleep at night? you never bunk in with us.'

'What's with all the questions suddenly?' Reeky replied in a rather prickly tone.

'I know what he does' said miserable Roger, 'he books into a posh hotel. Did you all know that he owns a Porsche? Bought it last year he did.'

Alex spoke up. 'Posh hotel? Porsche? How can you afford that? I've always wanted one of those. What's the secret?'

Reeky replied, 'Well, if you all carry on what you're doing and dedicate your life to working on these tours, then maybe I'll get another one next year.' I really don't know how he managed to drive away with all those empty cans and rubbish being thrown at his head.

Things settled down for a while and the talk turned to our future wrestling careers. At this time, I had already made up my mind to work on my gay-boy image, which I relayed to everyone, and I found their comments encouraging. Comments like 'Well it hasn't done Ada (Adrian Street) any harm,' and 'Ricky Starr has always been popular'. It was interesting to hear others' hopes for the future. Then miserable Roger buggered the conversation by stating that in his opinion, if this bloody tour was anything to go by, none of us had any future.

We were nearly in Weymouth when Alex said, 'Where are we staying tonight then Reeky?' Are we staying in the Salvation Army Hostel or on the streets in a cardboard box?'

'Tonight gentlemen,' said Reeky, 'you are staying at the La Rothier Hotel, run privately by a French couple. I have stayed there myself and can highly recommend it.'

'I shall treasure that recommendation Reeky, coming from you' said Andy, rather sarcastically.

On arriving at Les Digs, we were pleasantly surprised to find that it was quite pleasant, albeit very chintzy with net curtains everywhere and doilies where I'm sure doilies didn't belong, even the toilet holder was decorated with a doily. 'At least you will have something to wipe your arse with if the paper runs out' said Posh Keith.

We gathered in what was called the salon, which was in fact a front room, and had tea and cake. 'What are we going to do until pick-up time?' I asked, 'I mean it's not going to get too lively in here is it?'

'We are quite near the sea front and the tide is in, how about we hire some kit and do a spot of fishing?' said Andy. We all agreed except Posh Keith. 'If you think I'm going to catch and handle those smelly fish and kill them, you can think again.' It was Alex who said, 'Hey Keith, what do you think your father would say if he knew you were handling all those smelly fish?' Keith thought for a moment then said, 'Let's go get some rods then.' It was cold, windy and we got soaked and what's more, we only caught three mackerel between us.

On our way to return the kit to the hire shop, miserable Roger spoke up. 'If I was at home now, my missus would cook them in foil with a bit of butter.'

'If I was at home now my mother would give them to the cook to do it,' said Posh Keith. I gave the final statement. 'If I was at home now, I wouldn't be standing here, piss wet through, cold and smelling of bloody fish.'

We got back to Les Digs, had a shower and a change of clothes, picked up our wrestling gear and waited in the salon for our lift. we still had 45 minutes to wait so we managed to cadge some tea and coffee. We arrived at the hall and found the changing rooms, and very well appointed they were too, plenty of space, mirrors, toilet, shower and tea supplies

The wrestling went as it usually did and was well received by an appreciative crowd. If you have wondered why I don't go into detail about all the different bouts, there is very little to tell. We wrestled the same four bouts every night and already we were beginning to know what each other was thinking, let alone what move they were going to do next.

After the wrestling was finished, we did what we always did, climbed aboard the albatross and went back to our digs, wherever and whatever they may be. At least tonight we were hoping for a good night's sleep. And indeed, we all got one. We rose early, showered and packed our cases ready for a ratting good breakfast.

I walked into the dining room and stopped in my tracks. 'What the bloody hell is this?' Alex answered my outcry. 'It's a Continental breakfast.'

'What, no bacon or sausages?'

'Don't worry, we'll stop somewhere on the way and get a proper breakfast and Reeky can pay, it's about time that tight old bugger put his hand in his pocket. We are contracted for bed and breakfast to be provided, and we haven't had any breakfast yet.'

We made do with a few cereals and tea and prepared to leave when Reeky turned up. 'I don't know' said miserable Roger, there's always something that goes tits up, can't we have just one day when everything goes right?' ' There was plenty of time for that, after all, we were only halfway through the tour.

THE BOSTON CRAB

If you are a diehard wrestling fan, you will know that a Boston Crab is a well-known wrestling move. Well, I can tell you that I came across a different Boston crab. I was fighting in a venue just outside Boston, a place that I have never visited before, so I arrived in plenty of time, in case I got lost. There were no sat-navs in those days, so we had to use good old fashioned maps.

As I arrived early and the venue not yet open, I decided to get myself a coffee and a bite to eat. I was stood in a queue at the counter, just looking aimlessly around, when a woman further up the queue shouted at me, 'who the f**k are you looking at?' I was in a bit of a daze, and I wasn't aware that I had been looking in her direction.

' I'm so sorry' I replied, 'I was just thinking how attractive you are.' She giggled coyly and said, 'Oh! That's very kind of you to say so, I don't know what to say, I'm stuck for words.' I smiled back and thought to myself, I bet that doesn't happen often, you ugly, gobby cow.

The Lady at the Back

I was wrestling at Butlins' holiday camp in Minehead back in the mid 70s. I remember that the weather was hot and as I had arrived early, having travelled the relatively short distance from Taunton, I decided on a leisurely breakfast, a read of the newspaper and then a nice swim in the outdoor pool. All that would set me up for the day.

This venue meant that I had to fight twice as the show was put on for two different audiences. The first show was for the benefit of the second sitting for dinner, whilst the first sitting would eat, then the first sitting would come to see the second show and the second sitting would eat. I don't know who thought of that one, but it seemed to work. The shows consisted of two bouts in those days, and we would swap over opponents for the second show.

The promoter, who I shall not name, wasn't the most generous man, in fact, I think his brother's name was Ebeneezer, so we only got paid for one show. I was on second bout with a wrestler called

Terry Fear, from Bristol and secondly, I fought Cameron Cole from Gloucester. When I was waiting to go on for the second show, I noticed that at the back of the hall, opposite me, was a young lady in a wheelchair. I said to the promote who was standing by, 'That poor girl at the back in a wheelchair can't see with those big blokes in front of her. Shouldn't she be at the front?'

'Not my problem' he said, 'and not yours either. Yours is not to reason why, yours is just to wrestle and earn your crust.' I won't tell you what I thought, you can probably guess.

When it was my turn to enter the ring, I walked down to the ringside amid all the jeers and boos, then went on to the back of the hall on the other side of the ring. I said to the young lady, 'I'll take you down to the ringside so that you can see better. I must stop doing things like this, I thought to myself, as I put on the brakes, I will ruin my image of a villain if I keep being too nice, people might think I'm Cliff Richard.

The bout went well, and it was one of those rare occasions where I won on pinfalls. I got out of the ring and pushed the lady in the wheelchair to the back of the hall again where her parents (guess) were waiting for her. She thanked me and then went on her way, hopefully, to enjoy the rest of her holiday. I passed by the promoter, who was shaking his head at me. I walked past him into the changing room and said, in a low voice, so only he could hear me, 'up yours.'

END OF PART ONE

PART TWO

MY FIRST TOUR

I am compelled to say that when Reeky was up in the ring and acting as Master of Ceremonies, he looked every inch the part. Dressed in a dinner suit with bowtie and a microphone in his hand, you would think we were in the Royal Albert Hall. It's just a shame that he still smelled like a dung heap.

I relayed my thoughts to Alex. 'Don't worry about that, it's going to be sorted, just watch this space and don't say anything to anyone.' I knew lex had something up his sleeve, but I didn't know what.

We were finishing a big breakfast at a roadside café on our way to Exeter, each of us were wondering what s**t the day was going to throw at us as we went on our less than merry way. I remember that it was our longest journey yet and eventually we arrived in Exeter and, wouldn't you know it, yet again we all groaned as we left civilization and headed out to the countryside. It was a good few miles before we pulled into a farmyard, and not for the first time. It was so far out that even Reeky was spending the night with us.

We soon realized that we were wrestling in a big barn for the benefit of the Young Farmers' Society. We were to be the first attraction of the night's entertainment starting at 6 pm, and when the ring was cleared away, there was to be a barn dance. That's great I thought, when we had entertained them, then they would entertain us, made even better when they provided us with free drinks all night.

Alex pulled Reeky to one side. 'Hey Reeky, where are our digs?'

'You are in them' replied Reeky. 'There are plenty of bales around and sleeping bags in the corner over there. We'll be given breakfast in the morning and the changing room is behind that curtain over there.'

Alex wasn't happy. 'What about the showers and the bog?' Reeky came back, 'There's a stone trough outside the barn and a Portaloo at the back.'

Alex relayed all of this to the lads. 'That bloody Reeky will pay for this and it will be tonight gentlemen, I promise you.' We wrestled that night to the most unruly and disruptive crowd of morons that we had ever met, possibly because they were mostly drunk before we had even started. Usually, the first bout lasted just over 30 minutes, but it was over in about half that time. The other bouts followed suit, and the ring was dismantled and back in the van in no time at all.

The crowd couldn't have cared less, as they all wanted to get on with the barn dance and get to grips with all those ladies in gaily coloured frocks, I can't say I blamed them. In fact, it turned out to be a very entertaining evening, even miserable Roger cracked a smile or two. The local brew, which initially tasted like sheep dip, became more palatable the more you drank. Yes, it was turning out to be quite an evening.

Time for a pee, I thought to myself as I went in search of the loo. It was pitch dark outside, so I didn't bother to go around the back and headed for the other side of the barn where I was able to see where I was going from the lights of the farmhouse. As I stood there splashing my shoes, I noticed some bloke further up standing against a wall, I tried to focus partly because of the dim light and partly because of the volume of sheep dip I had consumed. What's that in front of him? What is he doing with that bloody sheep? I blinked again for a new focus. It wasn't a sheep, it was a girl in an astrakhan coat. They were doing what comes naturally.

I finished my pee and went back into the barn. It must have been about 12.30 am when the band packed up and everybody left. The whisper went around us wrestlers, 'don't be in a hurry to get into your sleeping bags chaps, let Reeky go first'.

We sat around talking for a while when Reeky decided he was going to sleep. We waited for him to get down to his underpants and then at a nod from Alex, we all grabbed him and carried him kicking and shouting outside the barn and dumped him into the freezing cold water trough. 'Rub him all over with this flannel' said Alex, ' I've got some bubble bath here.' He squirted half the bottle into the trough. 'Perhaps he'll smell better in the morning.'

We left him to get out himself as we all went to bed. For a good 30 minutes we could hear him muttering and mumbling to himself as he dried himself with a towel.

The next morning as we all nursed our hangovers at the breakfast table, we were in for a surprise. The night before, all the young farmers and their women had had a whip round for us wrestlers, which turned out to be double what we were paid that night. The ring riggers had received their share before they left last night. What a great night it had turned out to be after all. I don't think Reeky agreed though, he wasn't talking to any of us that day.

It wasn't long before we were heading for our next show in Exmouth. Andy spoke out. 'The first thing I am going to do when we get there is to have a nice hot shower, that is if there is one, is there Reeky?' No answer was the stern reply, and a little snigger went round the minibus. Oh dear, I thought, we have really p*ssed him off.

When we reached our destination, it turned out to be the annual gathering of a rather large caravan club. Well, that's a first, I thought.

We were allocated a couple of large static vans on the perimeter of the grounds for our digs and just across the way was a big block of showers and toilets. We eventually found the ring in a large marquee next to the substantial shop and club house that did a good menu for meals. This was more like it, we all agreed. There was a swimming pool, which of course was out of use as it was out of season. For once the weather was on our side, although it was far from hot, the sun was out, and we made the most of it. There were three of us to each van as Reeky did his usual vanishing act. We spent the day lounging around, eating at the club house and chatting to some of the caravan enthusiasts.

The wrestling was due to start at 6 pm, which meant we would be in time to see the cabaret at the club house. It was a local band followed by a comedian and promised to be a good night. I have to say that the wrestling audience were great and stood us a good few drinks at the bar. That is one night that will stay in my memory for ever.

Our next venue was Plymouth, a lovely place indeed, although knowing our luck we would be sleeping on the Titanic in hammocks and eating ships' biscuits for breakfast. I couldn't have been more wrong; we ended up fighting in a hall in a place called Pennycomequick. Our digs, which were more like a squat, was in the attic of a three-story house with a brothel on one side and a rough pub on the other. We had to be in the attic because the first floor was only rented by the hour.

The crowd for the wrestling wasn't much better, mainly dockers and retired sailors who clearly had spent their youth spoiling for a fight. There was very little appreciation for anything or anyone that night. I must be honest and say that I couldn't leave that place quick enough. Nothing that I could put my finger on, just an underlying uneasiness all around.

The next day we were on our way over the border to Truro in Cornwall. It was a pleasant day as any day would be, after that fiasco in Plymouth, so we were in high spirits. We didn't know where Reeky had gone off to after the show last night, but he had clearly had a result as he was speaking to us again after his impromptu bath in Exeter. I had to admit that the atmosphere in the albatross was just that bit sweeter. When we arrived, for once, we were in the Centre of Truro, not a farmyard in sight. The venue was in an empty fish market right on the harbour front. Okay, it was cold in there, but I guess the locals were used to it. Our digs for the night were a small cottage about ten minutes away, and I mean small, but we would manage, after all when it came to roughing it, we were past masters. It was a holiday let and would be a lot cheaper out of season, so poor old Reeky didn't have to dig too deep in his pocket.

The evening turned out to have the biggest crowd so far. You couldn't hear for people chatting before the show. I guess they were a closed community and who knows, maybe even related. I did notice one thing that I had never experienced before, every time we executed a move, they all clapped and cheered, every throw we made, another cheer went up and another round of applause. When the two young ones left the ring, they got a standing ovation. 'God they're easily pleased' said Richie as they entered the changing room. It was the same every bout.

Afterwards they took loads of photographs, and we signed more autographs than normal. I got the impression that they must have been starved of entertainment in these parts. Still, we were not complaining.

We cooked our own breakfast in the morning, not the best but still tasty, then of course, we had to wash up, which came as a bit of a shock. We were nearing the last leg of the tour, with mixed emotions for many of us. It might not have been the best ten days of our life but certainly an experience that none of us are likely to forget.

It was when we were on our way to Barnstaple that the subject of the two young lads splitting up on the bill and wrestling with the rest of us came up. Reeky had no objections, so Alex and I decided to go on first as warm up, Richie and Posh Keith, Andy and Miserable Roger second and third and the winners to fight for the cup.

I could see that the two young ones were apprehensive but they appreciated the faith we had in them and so they agreed. It would be the first time they had not fought each other but we reckoned that it was the right thing to do if they were going to further their wrestling careers. The venue was the function room of a local football and sports club. At least we would be okay for showers, and there was a bar too, which boded well for the interval.

Reeky seemed to be in deep conversation with a member of the club committee, which seemed to last for quite a while, which usually meant a problem of some kind. We soon heard from a disgruntled Reeky that the amount of tickets sold were thirteen. What was the reason? Apparently, Reeky had sent them the posters a few weeks before and they were still rolled up in the office – no one had posted them around the town.

'Not our problem' said Reeky, 'it's up to them to absorb any losses', which was true of course but it's never good to wrestle in front of such a small crowd. However, the show must go on even if it was in silence. Talk about flogging a dead donkey, it certainly was an uphill struggle. We were glad to be going on the next morning to our final show in Taunton.

Our next venue was a social club, a spacious building with every amenity you could imagine, and our digs was a very nice B&B within walking distance. Could this be the one with no snags attached? Time would tell. Okay, we were not looking for perfection in all quarters but a good stab at it would go down well.

We decided to have a look around Taunton and maybe grab a descent lunch somewhere. We came across a Chinese restaurant that looked reasonable, and we ordered plenty of food because on this tour, we didn't know if we would be eating again before breakfast tomorrow. The food and service turned out to be excellent and we left for our digs with full bellies. Our host at the B&B asked us if we had everything we needed, 'Yes thank you, we are just going up to have a nap before tonight's show.' 'Do you want us to wake you up and at what time?' said the lady of the house, we agreed and said about 5 pm, that would give us enough time to have a shower. It was exactly 5 pm when we received our wake-up call with a pot of tea and a few rounds of hot buttered toast. Wow, what a pleasant surprise.

We set off for the venue about 6.30 as it was only a short walk. We were welcomed by the door staff and escorted to the changing room. Again, everything we needed was on hand.

At about 7.15 I popped out to see what the crowd was like; the hall was full to the rafters with an audience of all ages, and they were brilliant. The warmup bout had it easy because the crowd were ready to rumble from the start. What a cracking evening, could it be a case of saving the best until last? Time would tell. After the show we were in loads of photographs with the crowd snapping away and I don't think I have ever signed so many autographs at a venue before.

We walked back to our digs feeling on top of the world and what's more, there was tea and sandwiches waiting for us in the dining room.

We slept like logs all night and awoke to a lovely pot of tea brought to our rooms. Breakfast was not found wanting either and soon we were on our last trip heading for home. A few hours later we were in the pub car park in Gloucester and saying our farewells. Our tour had consisted of highs and lows (mainly lows), but one thing we all agreed on, it was certainly an experience. Would we do it again? Some said maybe, and others said not bloody likely, and as for me, I wanted to see how my future career panned out before deciding. I give the last word to Alex: 'Never again, a total cake and arse party'.

EPILOGUE

To Part Two

Moving forward 45 years, I'll give you an update of those who were on that tour with me. I have no idea about Reeky as I never heard from him again. I have enquired from my wrestling mates but to no avail. A couple of times I had a bit of feedback such as 'Don't mention that Alistair to me.' I never pursued it after that. I wonder if he still has the minibus, or albatross as we called it.

Richie: It was with sadness that we heard he had been killed in a car crash just outside Cheltenham.

Andy: carried on wrestling for many years and carved out a good career for himself. I bumped into him several times over those years and have met up again at one of the wrestlers' reunions.

Alex: retired from wrestling in the late 70s and has turned his back on it altogether.

Keith (Posh Keith) packed in the wrestling shortly after our tour. He made it up with his parents and has just retired from being an accountant.

Roger (miserable Roger) retired from the ring after a back injury, worked as a driver for many years, and sadly died of cancer seven years ago.

God bless them all.

Early Trouble

Now and again we would get a bit of trouble from among the crowd, sometimes because of a wrestler's antics in the ring where an onlooker would get so wound up that he just had to let go of his anger. This was usually nipped in the bud by other wrestlers who had been looking on, before or after their own bouts. This one that I'm telling you about was certainly a one-off, at least in my career.

It happened in a hall in Anglesey in the latter part of the 70s. All of us wrestlers were relaxing in the changing room when the MC came rushing in, shouting, 'Hey guys, come and see what's happening in the hall. It can't be anything to do with us, I thought to myself, we are not due to start for another twenty minutes, the audience had only just started to arrive. We all rushed into the hall, which was about a quarter full, and I was stunned at the sight before me. There were chairs thrown about the floor and about ten chairs broken and thrown in the ring. One of the stools used by the wrestlers to step up into the ring was on the top of the pile. I looked around and saw male bodies strewn about the floor. There were screams coming from the ladies dotted around in seats opposite.

We all stood there wondering what the hell had happened when suddenly the police arrived. We wrestlers all filtered back into the changing room after all, it was nothing to do with us. The police had other ideas. It wasn't long before there was a knock on the door and two policemen entered. 'We've come to get statements from you all.'

'What for?' we remonstrated, 'none of us were there, we were all in here.'

'Well, we might have to cancel the show as it looks as though the wrestling may have incited a riot,' said one bumptious policeman.

That was enough for Jack, one of the tallest and biggest wrestlers there. He slowly stood up, sauntered over to the policeman, and in a deep, booming voice, looked down to him and said, 'Do you think you're going to take the bread out of the mouths of my wife and children? because if you do, then you will be inciting another riot and it will be a bigger b**tard than you had out there.'

The policeman looked up at him, thought for a moment, smiled a weak smile and replied 'Well, as none of you were on the scene, we will leave it at that then.' they took their leave.

The wrestling did manage to go ahead about 45 minutes late. It wasn't until the end that we found out that it was the latest chapter in a nasty feud between two large and nasty farming families in neighbouring villages over a land dispute that had arisen many years ago. It was well known to the local constabulary, who would be called out occasionally when it all got out of hand. The promoter was concerned that the hall would not be available for future wrestling events due to the hall having a bar licence, and any incidents involving the police could put their licence renewal in jeopardy. It must have turned out okay, as I wrestled there a couple more times in the following months.

Unwelcome guests

It was one night in Hereford, and it was also Clive's birthday. Clive was one of the most enthusiastic ring riggers in the business. It was his job to transport the ring to the venue and with a small team to erect the ring and the lighting gantry for the forthcoming show. Most riggers would sit in the van and wait for the rest of the crew to arrive. Not Clive, he was straight in there, unloading everything and erecting it all on his own. Then he would put out all the chairs. Sometimes it was all done before his crew arrived, even though it was sometimes up two flights of stairs. He was a grafter, was good old Clive.

It was for this reason that a few of us got together and organized a birthday drink after the show in the upstairs bar. 'Thanks lads but we must pack away the ring and lights first,' said Clive. That was him all over, duty before pleasure. We organized for the other riggers to do this, stating that they, thanks to Clive, had an easy ride at the set-up that evening. They reluctantly agreed.

After the last of the audience had departed, we hit the bar. We were all staying locally for the night, within walking distance of the hall, so no driving involved. There were a few stragglers in the bar, one of them called big Eddie who was slightly the worse for drink, and entertained us with his jokes and anecdotes, joining in with us. Big Eddie turned out to be quite a character, a farmer who was in fact a bit of a legend and known by the locals as Billy the Fish. He wouldn't say why, and we didn't ask, one could only imagine. It could have been because of the way he smelt, but I couldn't help thinking that there was more to it than that. Being a bar in a town hall, they called time at 11.30 pm as the staff wanted to get home.

'Never mind lads, it's all back to mine, I've got the van outside, I'm sure you can all manage in the back, it's not far,' said Eddie. It was with great in trepidation that we were soon rattling along (and I mean rattling) in an old rust bucket, heading for somewhere out in the wilds of Hereford. We were not sure that he was fit to drive and thinking back to those days, I don't think the breathalyzer had been invented. After being thrown about like a lottery ball in a machine, we arrived at this secluded farmhouse miles from civilization. 'Here we are lads,' said Eddie as we strode up the path leading to the rickety old front door. 'Bo***cks!' Eddie shouted, 'she's locked the door, the silly old cow.'

He picked up a house brick and started to bang the centre of the door. 'Brenda, let me in you stupid sod!' he shouted. An upstairs window creaked open and down came a tirade of abuse with a few choice words thrown in for good measure, from dear old Brenda who made it quite plain that his presence, and ours, were not welcome. The window was slammed shut.

Eddie turned to us. 'Don't worry lads, I have my own key in the shed, I'll just go and get it.' In his absence, Bruce, one of the wrestlers said, 'I don't know what you lot think but isn't it about time that we did a runner?'

'Where to?' said another, 'we haven't got a clue where we are.' By this time, big Eddie was back among us carrying a big bloody chain saw. To our amazement, he started it up and proceeded to cut a big square out of the front door. It eventually fell into the hallway as he stepped through the gap, putting the chain saw on a table. 'Come in lads, the beers are on me.'

We followed him into a room that resembled the living room of that well known comedy television show of the day called Steptoe and Son. 'I'll get the beers' said our host as he left the room.

The consensus was that we would have one drink, then get a taxi back. 'This is one birthday that I won't forget in a hurry' mumbled

Clive, as our host re-entered the room with the beer. It was about half an hour later when I asked him if I could use his phone to ring a taxi as we all had an early start in the morning. A quick look in the phone book gave me the number I needed, which I duly called. 'What's your address?' asked the lady from the cab company, 'uh, I don't know' I said, 'okay then, what is the name of the house owner?' 'Big Eddie, that's all I know,' I replied. 'Oh I know him, A car will be with you in about 30 minutes, can you be at the bottom of the drive?'

We said our goodbyes and left, all of us feeling a bit stunned at what we had witnessed and all in agreement that it had been a bad idea. 'So, you have spent the evening with big Eddie then' chuckled the driver. 'He's well known around these parts, in fact, he's quite a local legend, but for all the wrong reasons.'

'We met him tonight at the bar in the town hall.'

'Yes, it would have to be that bar, he's banned from all the pubs in the area.'

Nothing more was said about big Eddie and for me, that old saying came to mind, least said, soonest mended. The night had been one of regret and as far as I know, it was never mentioned again in wrestling circles. We wrestlers have many memories about our careers in the ring and some of the antics we got up to outside of it, but that night was one we all wanted to forget. Including good old Clive.

Sailed down the river

I may have mentioned in my last book that we have wrestled in the Forest of Dean on many occasions in my earlier days. The two venues that come to mind was the village of Ruardean Woodside and the Miners' Welfare Hall in Cinderford. Both venues welcomed us with open arms, and we rarely bought our own drinks at the local pubs after each show. I wrestled there at least twenty times over a period of at least three years. We were treated like locals, even wrestling at local fetes and once, at a grand wedding reception. So it was no surprise when we were contacted to ask if a few of us wrestlers would be willing to enter the annual raft race.

We managed to muster five of us to enter as we were due to wrestle there anyway, later that day, on the condition that they could arrange for someone to build our raft as we all lived some miles away and, logistically, that would be impossible.

They hastily agreed, so it was entered in our diaries, some two months away. The day arrived and we were all there, early in the morning. Each raft had a different theme and yes, of course, ours was wrestling.

We had been informed of our intended theme some weeks earlier and had decided to do it in our wrestling gear. It was a warm, sunny day, for which we were grateful, as we were to close the afternoon proceedings with a few bouts of wrestling in the open air.

The race was scheduled to start at 1 pm, before the children's races at 1.45. Our raft had been constructed of old oil drums with a wooden platform and four posts on the corners, plus three ropes around to make it look like a wrestling ring. Whoever made it had certainly put a lot of thought into it.

A local celebrity was on hand to open the fete. It was that well known radio presenter of the time Jimmy Young. Among his duties that day were to blow the whistle to start the race and to award the trophy to the winning team. We thought it might be a good idea to board our raft in plenty of time to get used to it – we needed to.

Between us we had entered the ring hundreds of times, but none of them involved bobbing and swinging about on water. Eventually, we were all on board – well, all except Dennis who somehow got tangled in the ropes and went arse over tit into the water. 'Man overboard!' they all shouted, between fits of laughter. We managed to drag Dennis aboard, dripping wet and mumbling to himself, 'who's bloody silly idea was this?'

A few minutes later the whistle was heard, and we were all away. Well, most of the others were. Terry, who clearly had never been in the scouts, was still trying to undo the stay rope. I had noticed that all the other rafts were tied with one simple knot, but ours had about fifteen small knots, someone's idea of sabotage no doubt. Finally, we were away. Okay, so we were last, but we took it gracefully. I thought it would be a nice gentle float to the finish line. Boy, was I wrong. Despite the use of the two makeshift paddles, which were made from squares of chipboard nailed to broom handles, we were thrashing about like a goldfish in a schoolboy's pocket, trying hard not to hit the bank and getting the paddles tangled in the ropes that surrounded us. Then another splash as Terry fell into the water, taking one of the paddles with him. By this time, we were surging forward and spinning around, and Terry, who couldn't catch up with us, had decided to wade ashore.

A couple of slashes later and there were two of us aboard with one paddle between us. 'Bugger this,' said Bill, 'I'm jumping ship.' 'What a great idea,' I replied. So we took our life in our hands like Butch

Cassidy and the Sundance Kid and leapt together into the unknown, holding our noses.

The water turned out to be about eight inches deep. It was such a shock that we both fell over and got soaked from head to foot. Finally, we waded our way to the bank, where we turned and saw our raft disappear around a bend, downstream. Bill turned to me and spluttered, 'well, that was a fiasco, let's hope the wrestling show goes better.'

'I've just had a thought,' I said. 'It's not long before we start wrestling and we are all going to have to wrestle with wet clothes.'

I must say that the wrestling went well, even though the crowd might have had trouble seeing the action through the haze as we warmed up and started to steam. After the show, we gave a hand down with the ring and into the van. 'Are we heading for the beer tent?' someone said. 'Not bloody likely, I'm off home to have a shower and get some of those bloody tadpoles out of my arse.'

We all agreed that it was the best plan. We said our farewells and set off in different directions, with a final agreement that if they asked us again next year, we would all be wrestling in Glasgow that day.

Karl Heinz

Karl Heinz, like so many others of that era, started his wrestling career as an amateur at the AEI Sports Club in Gravesend in the 1950s and took a total of six years learning his trade. However, the bright lights of the professional ranks soon became a place where Karl wanted to be. After being trained by Smiley Evans, he had his first professional bout in 1964. Initially, he worked for the independent promoters and was billed as a German wrestler who was on tour, hence the name Karl Heinz. However, he had never been to Germany and to quote the legendary Master of Ceremonies and compere of the Annual Wrestling Lunch, Steve Lytton, you don't get many Germans who were christened Nobby Clarke. In the early to mid-1970s Karl, or Nobby as he is known, moved to Joint Promotions, which meant that he was now facing some of the top stars such as Eddie Capelli, Alan Sargeant, Clive Myers, Mel Stuart, Catweazle and Brian Maxine, to name but a few.

It was about then that he teamed up with another wrestler who was alleged to be his brother Kurt. However, they were not real brothers, although they had similar looks. The team, billed as the Riot Squad, toured the UK and wrestled some of the top teams of the day such as the Royal Brothers, The Saints and a televised bout on the 6th of June 1987 against Chris Adams and Pat Patton.

Nobby was also known to international promoters and throughout his career made tours of the Middle East, India and numerous trips to various European countries. With joint promotions winding down their workload in the late 1980s Nobby returned to work for the independent promoters and finally hung up his boots in 1994 after a near 25-year career.

He continues to keep in contact with his former colleagues and is a regular attendee to most of the reunions. He is always a welcome face when it comes to verbally re-living the good old days. I always look forward to meeting up with Nobby on every occasion. He is, without doubt one of wrestling's 'nice guys' and has always managed to keep himself fit and active.

Alan Kilby

Born in Sheffield in 1943, Alan had an interest in karate and amateur wrestling before deciding on a career in the professional ranks. A stint working as a doorman in the northern clubs at a time when virtually 'anything goes' gave Alan the toughness and savvy that would later aid him in his professional career. Alan trained for two years before turning professional in 1963 a time when professional wrestling was at its height in popularity. Due to this and the number of shows being promoted across the UK at that time, work was plentiful, and he soon found himself working nightly against Joe Keegan, Terry Jowett and Mike Dallas. However, it was not long before he was to team up with Mike Eagers and a few years later he was to team up with another deaf wrestler, Harry Kendall as 'The Silent Ones.'

Throughout the 1970 and 80s Alan was becoming more and more popular, television appearances soon beckoned, and he was becoming a regular on the small screen opposing such stars as John Elijah, Alan Dennison, Keith Howard, Blackjack Mulligan, Skull Murphy and Honey Boy Zimba, to name but a few.

In November 1980 Alan was crowned the winner of the ITV Wrestling 25th Anniversary Trophy, defeating Alan Dennison in the final of the eight-man tournament filmed in Chester.

Alan would also form part of the jets wrestling team alongside Tom Tyrone, Steve Logan and Pat Patton and they would appear in mini tournaments around the UK.

In addition to these Alan was also a tag team partner to fellow Yorkshire wrestler Big Daddy, sharing a tag rope with the heavyweight over 50 times throughout his career.

Championship gold was sure to follow for Alan and it sure did as he captured the British Heavy Middleweight five times between 1981 and 1984, defeating King Ben for his first title in this weight in 1981 and then on a further four occasions defeating Dave Finlay. Alan was also a five times British Light Heavyweight champion between 1985 and 2001, defeating Steve Logan, King Ben, Skull Murphy, Danny Collins and Ian Wilson.

Alan would continue working for Max Crabtree and Brian Dixon throughout the latter part of his career and would also form another successful tag team with his son Adam. The pair travelled the UK and had great success. He wrestled until the late 2000s when after a 40-year plus career, he retired from the ring but left his own legacy in wrestling and can be very proud of his achievements along the way. In 2017 Alan was inducted into the wrestlers Hall of Fame at the Bridges Reunion, receiving the award from Mark Rollerball Rocco. Alan is indeed one of the all-time legends of British wrestling and is a real credit to the industry.

Dwight J. Ingleburgh

In my eyes, this book would not be complete without mentioning a wrestler whom I and many other wrestlers held in high esteem, none other than Dwight J. Ingleburgh, who, in my eyes, was the daddy of them all. I first met Dwight, whose real name was Sam Betts, at the first Blackpool reunion when after a few hours chat, we found that we had much in common. Least of all, the love of Kenya. Sam had spent time there during his army service and I, on many safaris, much later of course. A pure gentleman for those that had taken the time to get to know him and a most fascinating person to listen too. It was after that first meeting that I knew we would become good friends. Unfortunately, Sam died a couple of years ago and is, and always will be, sadly missed by all who had the good fortune to have met him. I had occasion to be able to do a small woodworking project for Sam a couple of years before he died. Out of gratitude, he gave me a set of carving chisels as a thank you. They have pride of place in my workshop to this day.

To do the memory of Sam the justice he deserves, I include one of many write-ups that have been done which will give you more insight into his career than I could ever do. I express my thanks to Alan 'Hack' Bamber of Wrestling Heritage for his permission to use this here.

The small South Yorkshire town of Barnsley is responsible for having produced a remarkable collection of colourful wrestling characters over the years that have included a bald headed loud-mouthed French man, a villainous German, a handsome American and at least three gypsies. The American in question was Dwight J. Ingleburgh. Tall, bronzed and muscular, he looked every bit the touring Yank, with a swagger and a disregard for those bothersome British rules. He looked the part, until he opened his mouth that is. Dwight's Yorkshire accent would have quickly aroused suspicions that New Jersey wasn't exactly the place where he kept his summer clothes in winter. Home for Dwight was Barnsley, where family and friends knew him as Sam, though his birth name was Brian.

For twenty years Dwight travelled around the country and overseas meeting the best of the wrestling world. For those whose who watched wrestling on television the name Dwight J Ingleburgh remained unknown, because he never appeared on television and neither did he work for Joint Promotions. Not that he didn't have the chance.

Wrestling Heritage has frequently commented that many fine and successful wrestlers worked outside the Joint Promotion organization, and we can think of no better example than Dwight. His reluctance to work for Joint Promotions was the television fans' loss. Be of no doubt that even if his name has passed you by, Dwight J Ingleburgh was one of the big names of British post-war wrestling.

On numerous occasions members of Joint Promotions asked Dwight to come across and work for them. Whilst the opportunity for television exposure may have had an immediate appeal, all advances from Joint Promotions were firmly rejected. For Dwight it was a pragmatic decision; the independent promoters could offer more work and paid more than Joint Promotions. 'The lads that worked for Joint got themselves on the television but most of them worked for peanuts,' Dwight told us.

For Dwight regular work and decent pay was necessary as he and his wife, Sheila, had four children to raise, and like all parents they wanted to do the best for their youngsters. Dwight and Sheila were more determined than most parents to give their children a good start, because their own humble origins had instilled a respect for education, a commitment to hard work and a sense of decency and honesty.

As a child Sam Betts was part of a loving family, but as the youngest of ten children money was always in short supply. He took up boxing at a local boys' club and was paid for his first fight, on Professor Bosco's boxing booth, when he was just ten years old!

Boxing, doing jobs to help his parents who were by then in their late fifties, and all the usual distractions for a ten-year-old meant that schoolwork was low in his priorities. Maybe that is one of the reasons Sam and Sheila encouraged such a strong interest in education in their children. It seems to have worked, and both are justifiably very proud of the achievements of their four children, all of whom have gone into skilled professional jobs. Sam left school at fourteen. Times weren't easy in 1947 and for all the youngsters in Barnsley opportunities were limited and Sam got a job down the coal mine.

Around the same time, he began developing his boxing and wrestling skills at Charlie Glover's gym. In those days Charlie's gym was in Quarry Street, only moving to The Junction in 1956. Sam told us, 'Charlie Glover was a great man, a very hard man. Everyone in Barnsley looked up to Charlie.'

He worked in the mines for two years, moving to the steelworks when he was sixteen. A couple of years later Sam was on the move again, this time 'called up' to the Irish Guards. Throughout his service days he was able to continue boxing and represented his regiment many times.

Sam's body matured during his service days, and he was quite a bit heavier when he left. Throughout his life he has enjoyed physical labour, using it as a convenient way of keeping fit and improving his sporting prowess. Following his national service Sam and fellow wrestler Pete Herman joined the Merchant Navy and travelled the world.

Sam returned to Barnsley in 1956, around the time that Charlie moved his gym to behind the pub of The Junction on Doncaster Road. 'It was a small place with a fantastic atmosphere. The wrestlers trained downstairs, and the boxers were upstairs.'

In 1957 Chancellor of the Exchequer Peter Thorneycroft abolished the Entertainment Tax, which had taken 25% of all entertainment revenue. With the stranglehold of the tax removed Charlie Glover seized the opportunity to promote wrestling, and asked Dwight to turn professional and work for him. Sam jumped at the chance to get paid for doing something he loved. It was Charlie Glover's son Brian (known to wrestling fans as Leon Arras) who bestowed Sam with the name Dwight J Ingleburgh of New Jersey. Sam looked the part and very quickly he established himself as a regular on the northern circuit against the likes of Karl Von Kramer, Bert Craddock, Charlie Glover, Dominic Pye and Henri Pierlot. As an established regular at the Junction Dwight also trained several of the younger lads, including Bruno Elrington, Leon Arras and Catweazle. In 1958 promoter Jack Atherton began booking Dwight and his career and class of opponent moved up a gear. Although not a member of Joint Promotions, Jack worked in conjunction with the organization and his shows featured both the famous names of Joint Promotion rings and up-and-coming independent wrestlers. Jack Atherton gave Sam a new name, Bill Dunn, and big-name opponents that included Hassan Ali Bey, Francis Sullivan, Count Bartelli, and Mike Marino.

In the years following his return to Barnsley things also became more serious between Dwight and his sweetheart, Sheila Broadhead, and the two of them married on 29th October 1960. Although Dwight's wrestling commitments were by then taking him around the country he tried to make his way home every night whenever possible. It was a hard life. It wasn't unknown for independent wrestlers to work two or three times a day, and more than double that when working the fairground booths as Dwight and many others did during the summer month.

Moreover, Dwight had a day job for most of his career, and somehow found time to build his own four bedroomed detached house! 'I worked in the mines, the steel works, as a plate layer on British Rail, for a steel erecting firm, always physical work. I enjoyed it, and it kept me fit,' he said.

Dwight was always fortunate that his employers were understanding of his wrestling commitments and usually agreeable to him taking time off and working flexible hours. This enabled him to accept overseas work which included visits to India, Pakistan, Sweden, Singapore, Malaysia and Kuwait. The visits to India and Pakistan were the highlights of Dwight's career, where he was for some reason billed as German. One of the greatest victories of all was over the great Goga Pehalwan.

He also has fond memories of his two visits to Sweden, a thirty-bout trip with promoter Don Robinson, and the second with Jack Taylor.

Usually a good guy in the ring, Dwight told us of one night when he did seem to irritate one ringsider. It was a match in Scarborough, for promoter Don Robinson. An irate female fan attacked Dwight with her rather large handbag. It was Bessie Braddock, MP, a keen wrestling fan who was holidaying in Scarborough.

Whilst outspoken about those promoters who treated wrestlers badly Dwight was always keen to acknowledge the many good friends he had made through wrestling and those promoters who treated their workers well, amongst whom he included Dominic Pye, Jim Lewis, George Kidd, Joe D'Orazio, Tony Scarlo, Tony Di Marto and Don Robinson.

Dwight continued wrestling until the late 1970s, his last match being at the Civic Theatre, Doncaster for promoter Cyril Knowles.

Obnoxious Fans

In my opinion, the majority of wrestling fans are lovely people and we have them to thank for supporting us back in the day and giving us wrestlers the chance to be able to do what we all loved doing. Without those die-hard fans, the world of professional wrestling could never have lasted this long.

I myself have had many laughs and much light-hearted banter with fans of all ages who loved to hate us. However, there are always exceptions to the rules and a minority sometimes, would push things just a bit too far and had us mere wrestlers, snapping back. Of course, I don't mean that we turned to violence, or anything like, that would be more than our job was worth, and we would never have worked in the business again, to say nothing of other wrestlers turning their backs on us forever more.

Then, of course, there was the persecution that you may have to endure, and quite right too. If we did snap, it was always verbal, and the fan would know that he or she had overstepped the mark. One of the strangest things that happened to me was in Bournemouth, before the evening bouts had begun, when a sweet old lady came up to me and said, 'excuse me Mr. Glitterboy, I've bought you some mascara and a couple of tubes of glitter, I thought they might be of use to you'. I thanked her very much and gave her a big hug.

Later, when I was fighting, my opponent threw me, and I ended up on the canvas against the ropes. Suddenly, I felt a searing pain in the middle of my back. I quickly turned to see who had done such a thing and saw that same dear old lady sitting down again and putting a small metal nail file back in her handbag. I carried on with the bout, dripping blood on the canvas from what turned out to be a four-inch gash down my mid, to lower back.

When the evening was over and the crowd were dispersing, that old lady came up to me, all smiles, and said 'Lovely show Glitterboy, see you next time you are here, I'll bring you some more make-up'. My thoughts were, not if I see you first you cantankerous old bag. I just stood there speechless with my mouth wide open and a stinging pain in my back.

Many times I have had to stand there and listen to a wrestling fan whilst he, or she, lectured me about a fight that I had many years ago which I couldn't even remember, how they would have done things differently, and if I had done this or that, then I would have won the fight. There is nothing worse than listening (or pretending to) to someone who is spouting on and on about something that they clearly know nothing about.

I remember talking to a wrestling superstar, at a reunion, when a person interrupted us and proceeded to tell him of the mistakes he had made on some television bout, many years ago, and what he should have done instead. The superstar listened for a couple of minutes, then asked the man how many times he had stepped into the ring. 'Oh, I've never wrestled but I have followed it on television for years,' he replied.

The superstar let him have it. 'Well, when you have been in the ring as many times as I have, then you can come and talk tactics with me. Until then, you can just f**k off.' This was from a superstar who, as far as I know, had never raised his voice to anyone in anger, which just goes to show that everyone has a limit to their tolerance.

I mentioned the word 'superstar'. The difference between a wrestler and a superstar wrestler is that I as a wrestler could count myself lucky if I received work from one of the top promoters, whereas a top promoter could count himself lucky if he could get a superstar wrestler to work for him.

The other problem areas to encounter were a few obnoxious fans, usually in the bar after the shows, either at the venue, if there was a bar, or more likely, in a pub near to the venue. I have had a few altercations with members of the crowd who had just seen me wrestle. Most wrestlers have experienced it at some time, and they all had their own way of dealing with the situation.

My way was to buy them a drink and hope that they calmed down. If that didn't work, then I would try and reason with them. If that failed, I would turn the conversation to my advantage and get them talking about some of the moves that we wrestlers use, then I'd offer to show them my famous 'Wurlitzer move'. 'Never heard of that one, eh? I'll show you.' I would put them in a full nelson (from behind, my arms under theirs and clasp both my hands at the back of their neck, lift their feet off the ground and spin them round a few times.) Often, the drink would take over and they would fall to the floor. I had to step back quick, so that the beer that they had drunk a while ago didn't go over my shoes. If he was a lot bigger than me and it didn't work, there was always plan B – run like hell.

As I said at the beginning, these confrontations were quite rare, and the large majority would come up and shake you by the hand and tell you what a great night that they have had and couldn't wait until the next time that wrestling came to town.

Enough is Enough

Back in the mid 70s, I was wrestling at a venue in Redditch. I don't always remember the places I visited, especially those of fifty years ago. I do, however, remember Redditch, because the bed I slept in that night, in some rundown guest house, had fleas and next day I had a red itch all over my legs, arms and back.

However, I do remember I was fighting Pete Cordell, A good wrestler I had worked with a few times in the past. Whenever I found myself on the canvas (which was far too often,) I felt what I thought were bits of grit or gravel sticking into my back. I drew the referee's attention to it; the bout was stopped while the canvas was swept. It was okay for a while, then it started again at the end of the round. The canvas was again swept, While this was happening, I glanced out into the audience and couldn't believe what I was seeing. In the second row back, sat on the end, was a chap with a large bag of peanuts. He was munching away but occasionally, he would flick a peanut into the ring, much to his own amusement. At the end of the next round, I leapt out of the ring, walked up to him, grabbed the bag of nuts from him and emptied what must have been a half the bag over his head. I returned to the ring with a loud cheer ringing in my ears from those sat around him. They had obviously seen what he had been up to.

At the end of the round, I noticed two things, firstly that his seat was empty and that he had walked out, probably from embarrassment, and secondly that was the first time I had received a cheer. With my dirty antics in the ring, I always got boos during my bouts, so to get a cheer was a real bonus. It didn't last long though – before the end of the bout, it was back to the boos.

Working a Gimmick

In the world of wrestling there are heroes, the squeaky clean ones who would stick to the rules and were loved and cheered by the crowds. Their technical names were the 'blue eyes', whilst the villains of the day, who would wind up the crowds, pull every dirty trick in the book and eventually incur the wrath of the crowd and have them banging on the ringside canvas and sometimes baying for blood, were known as 'heels'.

I confess that I was a heel through and through, but then I had a good reason. I have never considered myself as a highly skilled wrestler, so I could never dazzle the crowd and impress them. I had to upset and annoy them to evoke a reaction. That odd punch when the ref wasn't looking but the crowd were, holding my opponent in a head lock and running his face along the top rope, you get the general idea. Often, you would get caught by the ref and receive a public warning and then perhaps another later. This would inevitably lead to you being disqualified and you would leave the ring to boos whilst your opponent took all the cheers and the glory.

My persona as a gay boy helped me a lot as I would be a figure of fun before I'd even stepped into the ring. You must remember, that, back then in the 70s, gays were figures of amusement. People laughed at performers like John Inman, Larry Grayson, Danny La Rue, etc. They were among the top comedians of the day with their catch phrases such as 'I'm free' and 'Shut that door.' If anyone tried that same gimmick nowadays, it wouldn't get any reaction at all. How things have changed, and quite rightly too. It is just as easy to get a gimmick wrong, or to overdo it. I remember trying to enhance my entrances into the ring by carrying a bag of glitter and throwing it all over the crowd. It seemed like a great idea at the time, but it didn't work.

I had complaints from the crowd and even the caretaker who had to sweep it all up and had a good moan at the promoter, who, in turn, had a go at me. So after one show, I shelved the idea, I quickly learned that if a thing isn't broken, then don't fix it.

The Beekeeper

In my early days when working for my first independent promotions, I encountered a wrestler who we will call Alan. He lacked experience, probably because he thought he was good enough, and wouldn't accept any help or advice from the more experienced wrestler and probably thought that he had nothing left to learn.

I always thought he was being a fool to himself, because, up to that time, he had no ring appeal to speak of. However, he decided that he was going to become a sensation overnight by putting on a mask and dressing in beekeeper's clothing. To my mind, a masked wrestler needs not only to have an air of mystery about him but a touch of menace and villainy, and Alan had neither. When you imagine a masked wrestler, their name will give a clue to their persona: the Outlaw, the Executioner, the exorcist, Doctor Death, etc. 'The Beekeeper' didn't have the same ring about it somehow. It reminded me of an old boy down the road from me who kept bees. He moved slowly among the hives, handling the bees very gently and with great respect. Not the image of a ruthless villain of the ring.

A few of us tried to tell him this, but he wouldn't listen. Let him get on with it, was the consensus among us lads. I remember him coming into the ring with his mask on and a beekeeper's hat over the top. He clearly couldn't see where he was going as he stumbled his way in, falling over and bumping into chairs. He looked a right pillock. Finally, he made it into the ring amidst the sniggering of the crowd. He was introduced by the Master of Ceremonies and started to take his normal clothes off. As he removed his beekeeper's hat and his mask came off with it, he reached down, gingerly picked it up and put it back on. The mystery of this masked wrestler was not a mystery anymore, and the audience started to jeer.

The fight started rather clumsily as his opponent held him in a side head lock, which he managed to get out of. The trouble was, he had left his mask under his opponent's armpit. He snatched it back and put it on again. It was turning into a slapstick of the Benny Hill variety. The audience were stamping their feet and shouting 'off, off,

off.' By this time, I was feeling sorry for his opponent, who had involuntarily become a part of this farce and was getting angrier by the minute. Thank goodness the ref had the good sense to stop the bout, 'Match abandoned' he announced, and both wrestlers left the ring. The MC further announced that each member of the audience would receive a voucher for 25 percent off the next show, if they would leave their names on the door. I returned to the changing room after watching this debacle and was followed by the two wrestlers, who were arguing among themselves. Apart from those two, you could have heard a pin drop, until the promoter came in. I needn't tell you the rest. Suffice to say that nothing more was heard of the beekeeper, or of Alan. Perhaps he retired from wrestling and decided to keep bees instead.

The Masked Mummy

In my opinion, and in the opinion of many wrestlers, The Mummy had the finest gimmick of them all back in the day. His name was Alan too, but worlds apart from the last one. When he made his entrance into the ring, you felt that he was the real thing. He wore a suit made of bandages, which I was to later learn was specially designed and made for him as a two-piece garment, and what's more, you couldn't see the join. Incorporated into this costume was a cavity at the front which he would fill with talcum powder so that when he got hit there, out would come a cloud of dust. All designed to enhance his performance. He was a brilliant wrestler and coupled with his gimmick, was a sight to behold and was always first-class entertainment.

The audience certainly got their money's worth whenever he was on the bill. Alan also wrestled as 'Tarantula' which again, was always first-class entertainment. I was fortunate to share the bill with him a few times in the past. I can't say that we were great friends but were certainly on nodding terms.

I started to chat to him about fifty years later at the reunions, we started to hit it off and over the next few years we became good friends. Alan always has a string of stories to tell about his long and varied career, and believe me, he is the sort of Gentleman that you could listen to for hours.

Another Country

I don't remember the exact time in my career, but I guess that it was earlier on when I was green and totally wet behind the ears. There were four wrestlers travelling north of the border to Scotland. I was the youngest of the group and had never visited this part of the British Isles. It was getting late as we pulled into a service station for a bite to eat before crossing the border.

The driver, who shall be called Pete, (as he turned out to be a well-known wrestler and I would rather not use his real name) said, 'We will need our passports soon so get them ready.'

'Passports?' I shouted, 'You don't need them for Scotland do you?'

'Blimey' said Pete, 'don't you ever listen to the news? It's a new law that came in about two weeks ago, haven't you got one?'

'Yes, but I didn't think we would need it.'

'Well, you do now lad. Have you other two got yours?' They both nodded.

'Oh bugger. Now what do I do?'

'The best thing to do is to try and hitch a lift back home and get it. We can meet up again in Glasgow tomorrow night,' he said. Just walk over the bridge, you may have to wait a few hours, but some truck will be going your way eventually.'

I stood in that cold lorry park for nearly an hour. I was freezing, hungry and dying for a cup of tea when Pete arrived. 'Come on then, we're ready to go.'

'What about my passport?' I said.

'Don't be so bloody daft, we were only pulling your leg, of course you don't need it for Scotland.'

I must confess that I had the right hump with these jokers for the rest of the journey, not so much for the fact that I was the butt of their prank, that I could take, but the fact that I was still hungry and had missed out on a cup of tea.

We had a successful stay of five days travelling and wrestling in Scotland, the first of many as I will mention later in this book. And I had found out that wrestlers are notorious in winding each other up. I made a mental note that I must get my own back on this trio of tricksters, and the first chance came soon after. On our return, Pete was kind enough to let me stay at his house as we were all tired from our trip. Now I knew his address, it wasn't long before he was inundated with the most useless brochures for hearing aids, double glazing, the latest in car cleaning gadgets, greenhouses, etc. etc. One down, two more to go.

The After-Show Party

On the rare occasion when there were four or more wrestlers staying in the same guest house, we would usually arrive back after the show and have a drink together. It was quite possible that your paths had not crossed for several months, and it might be another few months before you would meet up again, so it was always good to have a catch up when you could. Sometimes, the other guests would join in, and it would end up being a right old party. It was great when your digs had a bar and your hosts would put on a bit of a buffet, although these evenings were rare indeed.

One evening I do remember was attending one of these functions in Hampshire. The food was plenty, the drinks were flowing, and I chatted to everyone about everything. As a non-drinker, then I, with the hosts permission, would head for the kitchen and help myself to a welcome cup of tea.

I remember that it was a lovely warm summer's night, so I positioned myself near an open window and made use of the nibbles that were dotted around the room. I had never tasted these particular nibbles before and wasn't sure if I liked them. They seemed to be quite salty but then, so are peanuts. After consuming half of the bowl, I decided that they were okay, so I ended up eating the rest. Later, whilst chatting to our host, I happened to
mention those tasty nibbles, asking what were they and where could I buy some.
She looked at me in horror. 'How many have you had?' she asked. 'Nearly the whole bowl' I said. She started to laugh. ' They were not nibbles' she replied, 'They were cat biscuits'.

I was mortified. 'Don't worry' she said through her laughter, 'there's a litter tray by the back door but please don't pee on the carpet.' By the end of the night, the word had got around, and everyone knew. It took me a good few years to live that one down among the lads and for ages after that evening, I was given the nickname of 'Top Cat'.

Beware of What You Hear

There were many times during my wrestling career when I found yourself fighting at a venue I had never been to before, especially if I was working for a new promoter. In this situation, I would always leave in plenty of time as getting lost or being late for a show was never an option. Being known as reliable was paramount if you wanted to keep the work rolling in. Once I had located the whereabouts of the venue, and sometimes, your digs for the night, I would take myself off to the nearest pub to while away the time.

Often, the pub would be busy with wrestling fans, meeting up and enjoying a drink or two before wandering over to the hall. It was during these evenings that I got to hear about the many antics of my fellow wrestling mates, things that they wouldn't tell their own mothers let alone their wives, and no, I'm not about to spill the beans. I was lucky that they probably didn't know me from Adam and if they had seen me before, it would have been in my full regalia of lurex tights, feather boa and full make up. A lot different from my normal appearance. One night in Essex, the conversation was lively in the pub and ran something like this:

'I see you've got your handbag at the ready Phyllis.'

'Oh yes, I never go wrestling without it.'

'Who do you fancy clouting tonight then?'

She looked around to the poster on the pub wall. 'Don't know yet, there's a couple that I've never seen before.'

'What about that 'Glitterboy' one? He sounds interesting.

Sounds like a poof to me?'

Someone else piped up. 'Saw him a few years ago at Barry Island holiday camp. A nasty bit of work if I remember, I couldn't make my mind up if he was a poof or not.'

'There's a challenge for you Phylis, I bet you could find out if he's a real fairy.'

'I love a challenge, I'll let you know after, back in here.'

The banter continued as they scrutinized the rest of the poster. I left the pub and made my way across the road and into the changing rooms. As a newcomer on the bill, I was on first bout. As I minced my way into the hall on my way to the ring, I spotted Phyllis and her cronies seated in the front row with her handbag at the ready. I stopped and whispered in her ear. 'Hello Phylis, it's a lovely pub that you have over the road, isn't it, and no, I'm not a real poof, I have a wife and four kids at home. (I never really.) I gave her a quick kiss on the cheek.

As I entered the ring, I glanced back the red face of Phyllis staring back at me. I managed to wind up the crowd that night with several of them up at the ringside, banging on the canvas, hurling the usual abuse and shouting at the ref to disqualify me. All this time, Phyllis was sitting firmly in her chair. I really hope I didn't ruin her usual enjoyment as I wouldn't have done that for the world. I could have gone back over the pub for last orders, Lord knows what sort of reception I would have got. It was getting late, and I had a long drive home. So I guess we will never know.

The Dreaded Landladies

This is a tale that is not just familiar to me, as many that travelled a lot in the 70s would testify, certainly among the wrestling fraternity. Sometimes as we travelled to a venue and we were due to fight someone that we didn't know, it was not unusual to be slightly apprehensive. How big is he? what is his specialty? am I likely to pick up an injury that could keep me out of the game for a while? These were some of the things that went through your mind on the journey.

None of this was a worry, just concerns. The real worry and likely to cause sheer panic were when your thoughts turned to where you were staying and even more important, what was the landlady going to be like.

Now before you pass judgment, let me tell you that I have seen Landladies that would have dropped Frank Bruno with one lash of the tongue. Thank goodness it has all changed nowadays, but back then, look out if you were caught excessively misusing the cruet or seen to be having three sugars in your tea.

My personal view is that they needed to boss people around. They usually had a husband but wisely, he had got himself a job which took him out early in the morning and back home late at night. I could imagine that those who had no job would congregate in the nearest library for hours on end, which is why all librarians should be up for the Nobel Peace Prize at least once a year. Okay, maybe I'm being a bit unkind to that institution, after all, some of them were nice people, friendly – in fact some of them were very friendly.

It was noted that when you came back late after a particularly hard fight when all you wanted was a good night's sleep, only to pull back your bed sheets and find your landlady in your bed and hear that familiar whisper of 'That's alright luv, he's working nights'. I was luckier than most, I could play my trump card. 'I'm sorry Madam, I have a partner, and HE wouldn't like it.' My gay persona in the ring certainly came in handy at times like these and it usually ended in a cup of cocoa and a fireside chat, but thank goodness it never turned nasty. It had the bonus of being able to stay there again without being accosted.

Malcolm

I was wrestling in Birmingham at a hall that I had fought in many times and as on all occasions there I had taken a bar of chocolate with me. It had become almost a ritual, as the chocolate was for a very special lad who I had got to know over the years. He was introduced to me on my first visit there by his mother. 'Jackie, will you please say hello to my son Malcolm.' He was a lad of about 12 years old and was an avid wrestling fan. He always got very excited at the wrestling, the bangs, the bumps and the cheers. It meant a lot to him.

You see, Malcolm was blind. The second time I met him I took him a bar of chocolate and that's how it started. I think it was about the fourth visit when I was chatting to Malcolm during the interval and asked him if he still liked the chocolate. 'Oh yes,' he said. 'I take it to bed and remember all the good times I've had that night while I eat it. Whenever I smell chocolate, I think of you. You see I recognize all wrestlers by their smell.'

'Oh, dear that must be difficult, most of us smell of sweat once we have been in the ring,' I said. He had a little chuckle. 'I have a smell for most people I meet, and you are chocolate.' I often think of him and wonder what he is doing now. Of course, he would be in his early 60s now.

My Brother Peter

You may wonder why I am including my big brother Pete in this collection of wrestling memories. The fact is, that he too was a wrestler and instrumental in my own induction into the world of wrestling.

Let me begin by sharing the character of my older brother, and what a character he was and still is. When I was a young teenager, he reminded me so much of Private Walker of Dad's Army fame. Later in life he gradually changed into the one and only Arthur Daley in 'Minder'. Now as we both reach our twilight years, he reminds me of Claude Jeremiah Greengrass, portrayed beautifully by the late Bill

Maynard in that nostalgic series of Heartbeat. For those who can identify with all three characters, I need say no more.

He wrestled successfully for many years as Farmer Pete before turning his hand to promoting, mainly in the southwest of England. I am proud to say that I shared the bill with him on many occasions during those early days, although it was many years before I worked for his promotions, but then, I guess I was his younger brother. Of course, I do have many memories of us in younger days, like the time he talked me into entering a business venture with him.

One of the madcap ideas that he frequently had was when he decided that there would be a fortune to be made at... steel erecting. We managed to scrape together a few basic tools – a few odd spanners, a couple of ladders, a spirit level and a much-needed piece of equipment called a 'dumpy level' for checking the levels on site. That, together with a rusty old van, and we were steel erectors. The only small snag was that neither of us had a bloody clue what we were doing. It took us most of the first day to figure out which steel post went where from the huge pile of steel that had been delivered a few days previously, since neither of us could read the plans. With the help of a hired digger, we spent the next day measuring out and digging the twenty or so holes for the posts. Once the holes were dug and the bottoms levelled with concrete, we decided that the crane which was arriving on the third day would lift the posts into place and the quickest and cheapest way was to put the posts in the holes and prop them up with timbers and wait for the concrete coming next day.

It was on that day that the owner came around to see our progress. 'Where are you staying?' he enquired. ' Oh, we just get our heads down in your barn,' said Pete. I could see that he was feeling sorry for us. 'I've got an old caravan over yonder, if you like, I can get a tractor and bring it round on site. It's a bit crusty inside but with a bit of a clean-up it should be more comfortable than the old barn.'

We jumped at the offer and duly prepared a place for it at the side of the site. It wasn't the Ritz but at least it was habitable, and we moved our stuff in straight away. Our stuff consisted of two suitcases, a couple of sleeping bags and our tools.

The village pub was a five-minute walk away so with a good meal inside us and a couple of pints later, we headed back to our caravan to get our heads down for the night, and what a night it was. We had picked the windiest night of the summer. It could have been weariness from a hard day's work, or the beer that we had drunk (I could have sworn that it was only a couple of beers each), but we had a great night's sleep and never heard a thing.

The next day when we came out on site, we couldn't believe our eyes. Apart from four posts, the rest had come crashing down during the night with two of them narrowly missing the caravan. So that's why they concreted them in as they went. Lesson learned (one of many).

A few days later, when we were both knackered after a full day's work, it was the hottest day of the year, and we were well into our second week. Pete had noticed that the owner had a lovely large house at the top of the drive with a smashing swimming pool situated at one side. 'Let's wait until dark and go and have a nice cooling swim, he won't know if we are quiet,' he said. I quickly agreed, so after our evening trek to the pub, we were back by eleven and ready for a dip in the pool.

We sneaked up to the pool by way of the front lawn, having left our clothes in the caravan. It was pitch black, so we made our way slowly to the poolside and slithered our way in. It was bloody freezing but eventually after a few silent gasps we got used to it. We hadn't calculated how loud splashing water was. 'Bloody hell' whispered Pete, there's a sodding shark in here'. We quickly made for the pool side. 'It's okay,' he continued, 'It's a kiddie's sailing boat.' You had me going there,' I whispered abruptly.

Then suddenly, three floodlights came on. I shot out of the pool, up across the lawn and into the trees. It was a few minutes before the lights went out and I saw Pete running to join me in the trees.

'What happened to you, I thought you were right behind me?' I said. 'I dived in the bushes at the side of the pool, the owner had only let his two dogs out for a pee. I've just spent the last few minutes in a bloody thorn bush with two dogs sniffing my bare arse. I'm not doing this again.'

The upshot of the whole adventure was that it had taken us seventeen days to complete the barn at the price we had agreed, minus the cost of the digger hire, crane hire, concrete, plus our food and travel, to do a job that should have taken a week. It had left us well out of pocket, in fact the whole affair had left me about three hundred pounds down.

'I don't think we are cut out to be steel erectors,' said Pete. It was a couple of weeks later when I suggested that if we sold the van and the tools, we might just about break even. 'Oh, I've already done that,' he said. I replied with 'So where's my half share?' (I already knew the answer.) 'I've spent it' he replied with a chuckle. Well, that was Pete for you.

He continued promoting for the next few years and finally ended up renting the ring and lighting equipment to various other promoters, but mainly to Duke Badger and Klondyke Jake from the Midlands area when they were putting their shows on along the South coast.

Injuries and Inconveniences

Of course, there was always the odd injury. The nature of what we do determines that you are not going to get it all your own way and the inevitable happens. If you're lucky, it's just a pulled tendon here or a dislocated limb there. A problem at the time but as things go, they are easy to bounce back from in a week or so. Of course, there have been too many wrestlers who have had career-ending injuries. Apart from my early days before I learned how far I could push the audience and was knocked out by the good ladies at the ringside, I did okay apart from the rope and canvas burns which every wrestler gets. I felt sorry for the married wrestlers who received rope burns on their necks and had the job of convincing their wives that it wasn't a love bite. (Or was it?)

Rope and canvas burns didn't bother us – in fact you didn't know about them until you took a shower, when the stinging would start. It was never a problem though, it just went with the territory. There was one thing that was a bigger nuisance and that was if you happened to be a villain, or a 'heel' as we were called, you would occasionally get cigarettes stubbed out on your back and legs from an irate member of the crowd. Thank goodness smoking was eventually banned in the halls, along with all sporting venues and public places.

Alan Brown RIP

In the early days of my wrestling career, I naturally found myself working in a few halls that were local to me and apart from wrestling I would visit them regularly for other occasions such as parties, watching events etc. So it was that I got chatting to the caretaker of one of these halls, who was a keen wrestling fan. Alan Brown was his name. We got on well, to the extent that I would regularly drop in on him and have the odd cup of tea if ever I was in the area.

Gradually over time I worked further afield, and my visits became less and less. One day I happened to bump into an old mate who informed me that Alan had died suddenly. I was shocked and saddened at this news and checked the local newspaper for details of his funeral which, out of respect, I duly attended. It was a very sad day for all concerned. Memories of Alan came flooding in from all quarters and when asked I replied 'He was a good friend a while ago'. I didn't know anyone at the funeral so I didn't fit in with the usual mix. The crematorium was full, and it was (to use the old cliché) a good send off.

I was kindly asked back to the wake at a local pub which, as you would expect, was a sad but dignified occasion where the usual buffet was laid out. I chatted to the odd person now and then and after about an hour, gave the widow my condolences, I wished her well and took my leave.

It was about three weeks later when I was doing some shopping in our local town, I felt a tap on my shoulder. I turned around and found a bloke smiling at me. It was Alan. 'How are you doing, my old mate? You're looking well.'

My response was limited to say the least. 'Yes, well, I thought, err, um, it's good to see you. You're, er, sort of looking well too.'

Apparently, we talked for a couple of minutes, but I don't remember what was said as my brain had gone into meltdown. We shook hands and I think I said that I would drop in the next time I came to town. I headed for the nearest café for a hot sweet tea. I needed to think things through.

I was in shock. It didn't take long for me to realize that I had attended the funeral of a bloke I had never met but who had the same name. I'd chatted to his family, his friends and his widow. I had drunk their drink, munched through their sandwiches. All this at the funeral of a stranger.

I can smile about it now, but at the time it was a weird experience and yes, I did feel guilty for a while. I wouldn't wish that mistake on my worst enemy.

I did visit my mate Alan on quite a few occasions after that, but I never let on what had happened. He continued his job as caretaker for a few years until he retired and moved away to Cornwall to be near his daughter and son-in-law.

The whole episode did however leave me with a legacy that whenever I have the unfortunate duty of attending funerals, I always make damn sure that I have got the right one. When you get to my age, it is inevitable that funerals come along more often than they did all those years ago but every time I find myself at one, the episode of my mate Alan always comes to mind.

A Hair-Raising Experience

If it hadn't been for those dedicated people who loved wrestling, then none of us would have had the careers in the ring that we enjoyed all those years. My experiences of those fans were varied, from those wanting to shake me by the hand to those who wanted to shake me by the throat, those who wanted to hurt me and those who wanted to mother me. Often women would bring me make-up, lipstick, eye shadow, eye liners, even tubes of glitter, and ten minutes later they were hitting me with their handbags. Am I the first man who can never understand women?

Loads of anecdotes have been penned by the members of the audience about wrestlers in the ring, how they have been entertaining, loved and hated in equal proportions. If they had won, lost or indeed, often in my case, disqualified, somewhere along the line, it was well documented.

Very seldom, if at all, a member of the audience seemed to be unusual to say the least. However, that is just what I am about to do. It was about four years into my career, and I was wrestling in Taunton. I was first on and had the unenviable task of getting the crowd worked up and persuading them to drop their inhibitions not only for my bout but for those to come. The first round went well, and they had already begun to hate me and to boo and hiss at me. I took a sip of water, intending to spit it over a few haters in the front row, when one of them caught my eye. There in front of me was a rather rotund gentleman, blowing raspberries at me for all he was worth.

I nearly choked on my mouthful of water. He was clearly wearing a wig, which, in his excitement, was slipping to one side. I could do nothing but laugh out loud. I had to pretend that I was laughing at the pathetic and futile comments that were aimed at me from the other people in the crowd.

The second round started, and I managed to work my way through a further four rounds before my disqualification sent me back to the changing room, to the satisfaction of that baying crowd.

Those rounds seem to go on forever, as I couldn't take my eyes off the gent with the mobile wig. Every time I looked at him, it had slipped a bit more, he would straighten it up and away it went again. It never actually came off but from time to time, it got bloody close. I never told the other wrestlers about it until after the show as I didn't feel it was my place to distract them and yes, a few of them had noticed, as well as the ref.

Memories of a Car Park

This incident came back to haunt me a few years ago because of my last book. I was advised by my publishers that to help with the sales it would be favourable to do as many book signings as possible within the confines of a popular bookshop. They would advertise your attendance well in advance and on the day would organize your books to be sold with the advantage of having it personally signed by the author. If the author was a well-known celebrity, there would be a massive crowd in attendance. Not so in my case, as in the grand scheme of things I was a nobody. However, there was still a small contingent of readers who had either remembered the golden age of wrestling on the television or had a father or grandfather who had been interested, so by the end of the day I should have signed enough books to make it worthwhile.

On this occasion it was a relatively small bookshop in Wiltshire. I arrived as arranged at 10 am and was due to start signing from 11 until 2 pm. I was warmly welcomed by Terry, the Manager, and his chief assistant Maureen, who promptly instructed a young salesgirl to make me a cup of tea, which I would really like to say was written in the contract, but no such luck. I only got that because on arrival I asked if there was a café nearby as I was gagging for a cup of tea.

Having arrived, they were not going to let me out of their sight, at least not until they had sold enough books to at least get their money back. They were pleasant enough. They stood either side of me as I sat at the desk surrounded by my books and a pen in my hand. We were all smiles as the photographer from the local paper snapped away while his less than enthusiastic friend asked a few questions about the book to accompany the photo in that night's edition.

The local press taken care of, it was time to open the doors to let in the vast crowd that had gathered, so they opened the door and let them both in... okay, it was a slow start, but the customers did trickle in over the next two hours. Women and men, young and old appeared and left, each clutching a signed copy of my book. The shop itself was doing a good trade generally, selling all types of books to all types of customers. The day was going nicely when a dear old lady came up with my book, the manager still on my right and his assistant on my left. She gave us all a big toothless grin. 'Can you sign it to Brenda please?'

'Of course Brenda' I said and signed it 'to Brenda with love from Martin. R. Gillott AKA The Glitterboy.' She smiled another toothless smile and said 'you don't remember me, do you?' Most fans would know more about my career than I did. She insisted on telling me where and when I had fought, who it was with and what the result was and all about a fight that I couldn't even remember. I braced myself. 'I'm afraid I don't, Brenda, enlighten me.'

'It was in Cheltenham Town Hall in 1975' she stated. 'You sh**ged me in the car park.' There was an awkward silence as the manager and his assistant walked away in different directions. To say that I was totally embarrassed was an understatement. 'Did I?' I stammered. 'You did' she answered and waddled out of the shop. It was the longest 50 minutes of book signing I have ever experienced. The manager thought it was hilarious. I don't know what his assistant thought as I never saw her again.

My Favourite Guest House

I had been looking through my list of engagements for the forthcoming month and I noticed that I was due to wrestle in South Wales for five consecutive nights. I didn't fancy all that driving to and back home every night, so I decided to stay in Wales throughout. I remembered a place that I had stayed at near Chepstow on a week's trip with my school, many years before. It was a big, rambling old house called 'Lindors' with a large, open fire and oak panelling throughout, with oak beams above. I was 13 years old at the time and still have fond memories of that place.

At that time, it was run by the Methodist Guild and was popular with many a weary traveller who occasionally needed a retreat. It was open also to non-Methodists, which suited me fine. I believe it has now changed its name and may have a bar serving cocktails, it may even be a gambling den, but I do hope not. Back then, it was a tranquil setting. Five minutes on the phone and I was booked in for six nights. It was located a few miles north of Chepstow, in a rural village called St Briavels. OK, so it wasn't that far from my home in Gloucester, but it was the Welsh side of the Severn Bridge, and the bonus was that it was on the edge of the Forest of Dean, which, as I have mentioned, is an area that I am particularly fond of.

In my opinion, it's nice to mix business with pleasure on the odd occasion. When the day arrived, I made the short trip to 'Lindors'. It was pleasant to find that the place had hardly changed and for a moment there, I was thirteen years old again.

My first fight that night was in Chepstow and the following night in Cardiff, which meant that I had two whole days to myself. The first day I spent wandering around visiting various places of interest and the second day was spent in the forest, paying particular attention to avoiding any wild boar that might be around. I had heard that they are dangerous and didn't like to be disturbed, so I was thankful that I didn't see one.

Wrestling a twenty stone opponent was one thing but facing a wild boar who didn't know the rules, forget it.

I ambled my way back to the guest house to spend the next couple of hours sitting by a roaring fire, drinking tea and consuming a pile of hot buttered toast. Does it get any better than that?

The following days were much the same apart from having to travel further to the venues. The last one was in Swansea and the furthest away, so I had to have my tea and toast earlier that day. All in all, it had been a great week. When I returned home and did my sums, I found that I had spent rather more than I had earned, but it was worth it. I thought to myself, I'll just call it a holiday. I have been back to 'Lindors' many times after that, the last time being about fifteen years ago, and what's more, I wouldn't be adverse to another weekend away, I would recommend it to anyone providing that it has retained that old worldly charm. It has been renamed Dean Valley Manor.

Not To Be Sniffed At

I am at the stage in writing this book where I am wondering if I should have entitled it 'How to make yourself look stupid', which as you will have read in the last two stories is probably a more apt title. This next tale is no exception. It concerns a young chap I met in 1971 at HMS Raleigh in Cornwall. He was only a couple of weeks into his basic training in the Royal Navy. Unfortunately for him, his brothers were high-ranking officers, and his father and grandfather had been higher ranking. If my memory serves me correctly, they were somewhat akin to Admiralty. This young lad was James from Chichester who had joined the Senior Service as a humble Junior Seaman, the lowest of the low. It must have been his father's wishes that young James would start at the bottom of the ladder and make his own way up the greasy pole to become officer material and beyond.

I came across James when he was being bullied by his newfound shipmates because of his background. I stepped in and fought his corner, as to me, any form of bullying is unacceptable at any level. Consequently, we became friends, and I was invited to stay with him and his family during his next leave. That is why I found myself in a lovely spacious and grand house in Chichester as guest for the weekend. They welcomed me with open arms and of course his mother was pleased to have her youngest boy home for a couple of days.

James insisted on showing me the sights of Chichester and we ended up at a sailing club. It was a lovely place and clearly you had to be a person of a certain standing in life to become a member. James signed me in, and we spent a pleasant couple of hours in the pure opulence of the Members' Bar. What was clear to me was that I was totally out of my depth in such surroundings whilst James was welcomed as a returning hero. A far cry from his billet on his naval base.

For the first time it occurred to me that although we came from totally different backgrounds, we could still be mates. We left there and finally made our way back in plenty of time for dinner, which in my world was at 1 pm but in his world was 7.30 pm. We had a couple of hours to wait so, with their leave, I went for a lie down, as the previous week I had been laid up with a bad cold and although I was no longer contagious, it had left me quite weak and lethargic.

After a sleep I was feeling quite recharged, so I dressed and went down to dine. It was a convivial evening, and the conversation was lively. We had got to that stage in the evening when the meal was over and the cigars and port were served. The ladies had left the room and the men's talk turned to the Navy. Just as the conversation had reached the great naval battles of history, most of which went over my head, I sneezed.

Now I don't know how best to explain the results of this sudden action, but it was everywhere. All over both sleeves, down the front of my best dinner jacket, over the tablecloth, everywhere. I picked up my napkin and mopped it up the best I could. The silence from around the table was uncomfortable to say the least.

I made my excuses and apologies and retired to my room, via the bathroom of course. I didn't sleep well that night, out of shame, I think. Breakfast next morning wasn't too bad as I only had James for company and anyway, it was soon time for my train. I said my thanks and goodbyes to all concerned and James drove me to the station. The previous evening's catastrophe was not mentioned, so as I shook hands with him, I asked him if my previous night's cabaret had been mentioned by his folks. He told me not to worry, it wasn't a problem, and nothing was said except for his grandfather who upon my hasty departure just raised his glass and said, 'Well we should all be grateful that the boy never had the Bombay trots'.

I never saw him after that, as I carried on with my wrestling career and as far as I can guess, he probably made it to the top in Her Majesty's Royal Navy. I can just picture him now, Admiral Sir James RN sat at the head of his own table in his own large house somewhere, wondering what sort of waif and stray his own grandson has brought home this weekend.

With A Little Help From My Friend

It was high summer in the early part of the 1970s and at that time of year the wrestling bookings tended to drift towards the coastal areas. Not only the many holiday camps that were around at that time but in the town halls in the most popular resorts. That day we were in Lyme Regis. I had travelled down with our lorry driver Bryan, whose job it was to transport the ring; others would be coming by car.

We arrived in plenty of time to set up and put the chairs out. The Promoter that day was Duke Badger from Birmingham ,who travelled down with Klondyke Jake. The evening went well, and I noticed a couple of young ladies were hanging around afterwards as we dismantled the ring. I later heard that they were locals and apparently one of them had taken a fancy to me. Okay, I was young and so was she. It was the 70s, an age of promiscuity. What should I have done? What would you have done in my position?

Being local, they knew the best place to get food at that time of night so off we set to a nearby transport café. My older brother Pete had been on the same bill that night and had brought his large Mercedes, so this young lady and I jumped into the back seat to get to the café. We were the first to arrive and brother Pete went to get some food and left us in the back seat.

I guess you know what came next. I seemed to be doing well, and I was feeling like Superman that night. Well at least I was until I looked out of the window to see Klondyke Jake with his shoulder to the car, was rocking it for all he was worth. Ah well – at least she never noticed that I wasn't Superman. Thanks Jake, but I could have managed. Honestly. He never let me forget that night. Good old Jake, always there when you wanted him, and when you didn't.

Championing the Cause

As a wrestler we get asked many questions, which most of us are more than happy to answer. But there is one statement often said about us that really annoys me and many others like me. When someone says 'I bet you were a right bully at school,' I feel duty bound to put them right. I was never a bully, and I could never be one. In fact, I spent my earlier school years standing up to bullies. I learned early in life that I was fortunate to have very little fear. Do not think that bullying stops when you leave school because in my experience, it doesn't. The fact that I had little fear meant that I would stand up to them knowing that the worst I would get is a good hiding. It never came to that.

The best put down of bullying I ever heard came later in my life when, in my early wrestling days, I would do a bit of work on building sites to make up the money to live. This day as we all sat around in the sun at lunchtime, one young lad who fancied himself as a hard nut kept annoying one old boy who was in his 60s. He said to him 'Hey Sid, can you fight?' Sid took his pipe from between his lips and replied 'Nope. But I can make it bloody difficult for them that think they can.'

We were in hysterics, which embarrassed the youngster and shut him up for the rest of the day. I have never met any old school wrestler who could be labelled as a bully. As one wrestler friend of mine put it, 'We were paid to fight. Not made to fight.'

QUESTIONS I'M OFTEN ASKED

I think now is the time when I answer a few questions and take you behind the scenes, as it were. Please remember that the answers are only my opinions. Bear in mind that I am not an authority in the world of wrestling, and there are a lot of excellent historians out there whose opinions are of more value in the grand scheme of things.

Their answers have been researched, mine are based on an ever-fading memory. I will pass on the obvious question, 'Is wrestling fixed?' I dealt with this one in my last book. Nowadays, if I am asked that question, I always make the same statement. ' Does it really matter? We all know that John Wayne wasn't a real cowboy, but that didn't prevent us from enjoying the film. In my opinion, that will suffice.

Q1. Is it true that some wrestlers travelled around together?

Yes of course it is. And why not? A lot of cynical people think that if wrestlers travel together then the result must be rigged. Let me step to one side and talk about the legal profession. It is sometimes the case that two barristers find themselves in court acting against each other. It is on the cards that they may travel together, stay in the same Hotel, eat and socialize together outside the courtroom.

They may even work in the same Chambers yet spend their working day trying to tear each other to bits in the courtroom. When the case is over, they may well travel back home together. The best of friends. Can you get a more honourable and distinguished profession than the legal profession? The parallel is exact. To use one of their sayings, I rest my case.

Q2. Do you get prefight nerves?

Sometimes, but it was never to do with the art of wrestling itself. It was more likely to be what the crowd was like or how they would take you that evening. I was lucky in that by the time I entered the hall and got into the ring I had done a fair bit of mincing and turning my nose up at the crowd, pranced around and preened myself, the crowd had already let me know in no uncertain terms what they had thought of me. I was never nervous at getting in the ring although I had a few near escapes getting out and back to the changing rooms. I guess some of them wanted a keepsake of me. One wanted my arm another wanted my throat etc.

I knew some wrestlers who would pace up and down in the changing rooms full of nerves and others who were so relaxed you almost had to wake them up to go on. I spent a fair bit of time getting ready and by the time I had put my make-up on, glued many sequins onto my face, covered myself in glitter and generally made myself pretty, the time just went, and I was on my way.

Of course, you would be more nervous when you were working for the first time with a new promoter because you had the additional pressure that if you didn't do your job properly then you might not get to work for him again and that could affect your workload in the future.

Q3. Which were your best and worst venues?

This is a difficult question because it depends on what you want out of a venue. For your average wrestler a venue is just a venue, the same as a ring is just a ring. I know that some reckon a good venue and a bad venue depend on how near the nearest pub or Chinese restaurant is situated. For others it is parking or maybe the distance they must travel. For me, it would depend on how well we were looked after. As I remember it, my best one was in the Forest of Dean in Gloucestershire. they probably looked after us well as it was a charity evening, and we were giving our services free of charge.

When we arrived, we had our own parking spaces just outside of the sports hall. Our heated changing room consisted of plenty of space to change, plenty of mirrors, a television in the corner, Hot showers with plenty of towels at hand and a very generous buffet laid out with tea and coffee on tap. And for those who wanted them, quite a few cans of beer. Believe me, it doesn't get better than that. I don't remember how the wrestling went but the facilities would have taken some beating and it has stayed in my memory for all those years.

I think the worst one was up in Fishguard when we wrestled in a large cold hangar of a building that was a fish market by day and an entertainment venue by night. I think I may have mentioned this one in my last book. It was so cold that the crowd had their coats on all night. Showers? Not a chance. We made do with a bucket of cold water and a wet sponge. The changing area was behind a temporary curtain made of smelly muslin and there were two chairs. It was so cold that I swear that as I was putting on my make-up the lipstick backed into the tube. I was glad to get back to the digs and a warm shower.

I don't recall any other wrestling evenings happening in that venue. Perhaps the promoters thought better of it and changed to somewhere more suitable.

Q 4. What are your views on modern wrestling?

I think it's great. Of course, I think that as a wrestler in the 70s we had the best times but then, I would say that wouldn't I. There are a lot of good wrestlers earning a crust today and I would like to say thank you for keeping the game alive. Without it, wrestling would have died out years ago. It's changed a lot, but it had to. It is bringing the sort of entertainment that people want now. I have some good friends who are modern wrestlers and believe me the enthusiasm is there just as it was in our day.

I have also had the pleasure of meeting and chatting to some of them at the many wrestling reunions that I attend. They are always respectful for what we achieved in our time, and I believe that at the very least we should show our respect for them.

The one thing that I don't understand is, in our day, if you had won a championship belt then that was viewed by all as a major achievement, but the trend seems to be now that most wrestlers appear to have at least one and often they appear to have three each.

I don't quite know how it works, perhaps someone out there can enlighten me.

Q5. Who were your wrestling heroes?

This is a great question and one that I have been asked many times. I don't think 'hero' is the right word. Inspiration is probably a better word. Who inspired me? There were three that come to mind, but if I really sat and thought about it there would be enough to fill a book on this one subject. The first one that inspired me, and I have no doubt inspired many was George Kidd. I often thought that if I had attained a tenth of the skill that he had, I wouldn't have needed a gimmick. I could have impressed the crowds instead of having to rely on my persona to do the business. I guess that if you had ever seen this man in action then you will know exactly what I mean. I only ever saw him once and that was when I was younger, and he had a charisma in the ring that most could only dream of. I remember thinking, wow, I just so want to be a wrestler. My second inspiration was the late and great Pat Roach, the gentle giant who commanded and indeed got the respect he deserved. He helped me more than he ever knew when I was starting out in the business. When he spoke, you listened. There was always a lot to learn from him and he didn't mind giving any young wrestler sound advice that he thought would be useful. It always was. I was fortunate to become good friends with Pat over the years and trained with him (or should I say under him) and of course met up with him in and out of the ring for many years. I kept in contact with him long after I hung up my boots and it was a very sad day when he went to the great dressing room in the sky.

Third on my list but by no means least, is my old mate Johnny Kincaid. He was what I call a wrestler's wrestler, a great all-rounder in the ring and a thoroughly nice bloke out of it. He was also a great travelling companion. (More of that later.)

We all have heroes in life and just because I was a wrestler, I was also a fan. I did my bit of watching it on the television and then in the flesh whenever and wherever I could. If it hadn't been for those who went before, I would never have had the inspiration to get up and have a go. I for one am very glad that I did.

Q6. Are you interested in any other sport?

Nowadays, the only sport I watch is on the television and of course it is football, but only when the ladies are playing. In my opinion, when the ladies play, it is sport and proper football, when the men play, it's a business. They seem to try every trick in the book to get a free kick or better still, a penalty. This to me makes good business sense but makes for boring football. The ref blows his whistle more than Herb Albert blew his trumpet.

People say why don't we win the world cup? In my humble opinion it seems that we buy in a lot of players from abroad at extortionate cost to the club, which is all fine until a World Cup is played out, then they all go home and play for their own country, and we are left with very little talent. Don't shoot me, that's only my opinion.

Before all my mates lynch me, I have nothing against men's football, it's just not for me. I like to see a bit of sport, and if the ladies swapped shirts after the game, you wouldn't get any complaints from me.

The Man Behind the Mask

The concept of a masked mystery man has for many, many years been a mainstay of professional wrestling, indeed a feature known only, legitimately, in this walk of life. It is not difficult for wrestling fans to appreciate that a small group of career hooded wrestlers who assiduously guard the mystique of the tradition, letting it be known that they would unmask if ever beaten and never allowing themselves to be seen without their masks on, decline most interviews. We think of The Black Mask, Count Bartelli, Doctor Death, The Zebra Kid. We acknowledge the professionalism of the shorter-lived reigns of The Outlaw, The Exorcist and The White Angel. And we give a nod to European greats, L'Ange Blanc and Le Bourreau de Béthune.

Arguably, however, the biggest name of them all remains paradoxically one of the wrestlers we know most about. Kendo Nagasaki. His 30+ years of activity can be broken down quite neatly into clearly defined eras. A somewhat unheralded start at the end of 1964 saw him gaining experience in supporting heavyweight bouts and tagging alongside Count Bartelli. Perhaps the peak of his fame was achieved a year and a half later, when, after publicly falling out with Bartelli in a tag match against Tibor Szakacs and Henri Pierlot, a challenge match was arranged between the two mystery characters. Count Bartelli may well have been relieved finally to dispense with his mask after 26 years behind it, but youthful Nagasaki was still growing in stature and the claiming of such a notable scalp helped him on his way.

Above they are seen during the preliminaries of that momentous 1966 bout. The late sixties saw Kendo Nagasaki appearing regularly all over the UK, debuting at the Royal Albert Hall, but, like Bartelli before him, still denying any television coverage. The Outlaw and the Zebra Kid did appear on television, so we must look elsewhere for a reason why Nagasaki didn't.

The Second World War was still fresh in the minds of many and perhaps a stereotypical Japanese sword bearer, clad in samurai garb and menacingly wielding Japanese steel, was one chance too many to take for the authorities and the cautious promoters. Remember that even the genteel Dad's Army was considered potentially disrespectful before its first 1968 showing.

But there was another respect in which Nagasaki was overlooked. The annual Royal Albert Hall Heavyweight Trophy was the pinnacle of the year, a great honour to participate in and an annual grouping of 8 great wrestlers. Tibor Szakacs and Gordon Nelson spring to mind as international stars who were able claim honours in the UK thanks to the open nature of the event. But Nagasaki never got a look in. Surely this would have been an ideal platform for him to gain greater notoriety.

On the other hand, he had such a breathtakingly innovative gimmick that no further honours were necessary, and he did enjoy the not inconsiderable benefit of being required to remain unmasked against all the great heavyweight opposition of the day, including four 1969 victories over Jean Ferre. The authorities finally relented and on Cup Final Day 1971 the nation caught its first televised sighting of Kendo Nagasaki, though the sword ceremony was deemed too frightening, and we only caught the final few rounds of a quiet victory over Wayne Bridges. Still, the horizontally barred mask was enough to establish the curiosity of the television public, even though the terror of what we had already been witnessing at our local halls for many years now lay ahead.

1971 was a key year indeed. Now Nagasaki had his tv breakthrough, he was determined to make the most of it, and the opportunity didn't slip from his grasp. After a couple of follow-up bouts within World of Sport, a sensational match was aired from Catterick Bridge against Bristol's Billy Howes and in which the strangely shaven and tattooed head of Kendo Nagasaki was seen for the first time.

Controversy reigned, had Nagasaki been beaten? Who was in fact disqualified? Had he unmasked voluntarily? No matter, Nagasaki's days in main supporting bouts were now over and he toured the land, his evil and mysterious reputation greatly enhanced. At the end of the year, we were in for a further shock when, at our local halls, a loquacious sideburned manager appeared with Nagasaki, to present him before each bout. George E. Gillette was a sadistic and arrogant in-ring speaker but proved popular with fans, orchestrating their fascination, distributing photos and making sure that everyone got a coveted autograph.

In short, contact, albeit indirect, was now established with the silent one, the two disappeared off to Calgary at the end of the year and met with success at the North American Open Championship. As far as we can see this was only Nagasaki's second stint overseas after a short 1968 summer in Japan, where he wrestled under a different name. Six months later and Nagasaki and Gillette were back, and we can safely say that Kendo Nagasaki's heyday continued for the next couple of years. In this time, he faced and sensationally beat on television the hitherto unbeaten and seemingly unbeatable Shirley Crabtree, courtesy of a flying knee to the chin. But his main repertoire of finishers at this time centred around moves brought back from North America: the Rack, The Atomic Chop and the Kamikaze Roll. Another legendary bout was the 40-minute Royal Albert Hall scoreless draw against Bruno Elrington.

The first 10 years of Nagasaki, therefore, amounted to a textbook professional approach, travelling widely, carefully preserving the many and varied aspects to his outlandish gimmick, remaining seemingly invincible, and making a great name for himself. Carefully staged promotional interviews and write-ups alluded to oriental training, and interests in Sailing, Chess and The Arts.

Quite what led to the events of the following years is not easy to determine, but events there were indeed aplenty. Disaffiliation from Joint Promotions rings started the ball rolling and denied Nagasaki television coverage, but the independent circuit, headed by a promoter in Jackie Pallo who at the time seemed headed for success, offered lucrative alternative bookings. It also allowed the opportunity for Nagasaki to gain titles, such as the WWF World Championship, won against Johnny Kincaid in Hastings in the summer of 1974.

When the independent circuit failed to bring the hoped for rewards, Nagasaki fleetingly retired for the first time. By the time he returned to Joint Promotions rings, his status was somewhat lower, a new headlining kid having emerged on the grappling block in the guise of Big Daddy. Nagasaki was now required to make the Halifax giant look good, culminating in a televised unmasking at the Yorkshireman's hands.

Many fans found not merely distasteful but rather silly the rubbishing of the carefully sculpted persona that was the rapid external development in Gillette's effeminate dress and the pair's open in-ring cuddling. By the end of 1977 it had all apparently become too much for Nagasaki and Gillette, and a televised Christmas unmasking of the ceremonial sword bearer was aired from Wolverhampton.

Who knows what their plans were, but just a few months later and Nagasaki was back again, this time wrestling maskless. His first televised bout was against Roger Wells, and we saw a change of style with Nagasaki wrestling cleanly. But this phase of his career was also unsatisfactory and soon fizzled out after initial curiosity value.

A year after this return, Nagasaki had turned his back on wrestling once again, and in a Daily Mirror centre spread was photographed with a rare smile and looking quite normal, alongside an article in which he lifted the lid on some of the tricks of the trade. After George E. Gillette's death, Kendo Nagasaki appeared with various managers, but none managed to strike a chord with promoters.

The development in these final years of the Kendo Nagasaki wrestling career was more to do with stories of faith healing, largely dismissed as irrelevant by most fans but no doubt designed with a purpose. The red clad combatant appeared increasingly in tag matches where younger partners could share the heat, but the great man was not averse to continued risk-taking in classic encounters with Giant Haystacks, Tony St Clair, Mark Rocco and others.

The one-off curriculum was an invitation for imposters. As well as imitation at home, the Kendo Nagasaki name was at best borrowed in the USA; the American version, wrestled without a mask. However, such was the athletic prowess of the original British version that only the most superficial of fans needed to draw upon the missing index finger for proof of authenticity.

For once we identify a career that did not fizzle out. The persona that is Kendo Nagasaki was so carefully crafted and delivered from its 1964 inception that we can be thankful that a wary marketing eye has guided it through the stages we have described to a present day where a dedicated website keeps the image alive and TV appearances continue right into the 21st century. Just one key mystery remains, and it centres around 1964. Who on earth dreamt up this outrageously creative gimmick? Who on earth trained this agile youth with the wrestling skills and mature aplomb to implement the gimmick so magnificently right from his 1964 début? Was Count Bartelli a key figure in Nagasaki's development or was he just an incidental player in that in 1966 he had decided his days behind the mask were up? Our insatiable thirst for facts as die-hard fans and respecters of all that is Kendo Nagasaki will ensure that we persevere unstintingly in pursuit of this final unravelling of the threads that secure the Ceremonial Sword Bearer's barred hood in place to this day.

Ladies of the Ring

I am frequently asked, and have indeed spoken often about, my views on women wrestlers. I have to say that it was mostly the local authorities that seemed to have a problem with lady wrestlers. I don't think I ever came across any wrestler that was against it. In fact, I seem to remember that the ladies were banned from wrestling for a while within the London area and there were a few halls throughout the country that would not allow the booking of their venues if the ladies were on the bill. I never understood why, when they were as competent and skilful as any male counterparts and in many cases, were better right across the board. I have to say that I have shared the bill on many occasions with these ladies and am proud to have done so.

I am also proud to be able to say that I have many friends who were great lady wrestlers of the day. Most people I meet nowadays want to talk about my wrestling days. Some can remember bouts that I have had and can even tell you who I was fighting and what the result was. Some probably remember more about my wrestling career than I do and there are others who can remember sitting with their parents or grandparents and laughing at them as they heard them shouting their contempt at the television set for what was unfolding before their very eyes.

There are a few however who wanted to know what I did before I took up the profession and how did I make a living at it. The truth is, I didn't. Well not in the early days anyway. Apart from my stint on the fairground boxing and wrestling booths which, in the grand scheme of things, wasn't a huge part of my career, I was forced to take on several jobs to keep my head above water. I would work during the day and then travel to various places to wrestle at night. I will now lay before you some of the antics I was forced to get up to in order that I could eat and survive so that I might follow my dream.

Into the Woods

The very first job that I took was in a family business run by a Mr Scrubey near where I lived. He was a man who seemed very old to me. I was 15 and I guess he would have been in his early 70s. In the past, he was a Master at his art and rumour had it that in his youth, he had been a member of an exclusive group of craftsmen that had built the Queen's dolls' house which I believe is still on display at Buckingham Palace to this day.

I am proud to be classed as old school, so he must have been absolutely ancient school and with only hand tools to work with, he was a fine craftsman in his day. It was just a shame that he was reduced to making cabinets for the early stereo speakers. No wonder that most of the old crafts are lost to us nowadays.

At least when I worked for him, his workshop had been modernized. Well, that is if you can call the roof space dotted with pulley wheels and large, long belts whizzing at great speed over your heads modernization. Each one would operate a particular machine. There were no on/off switches; to stop the machine, you would have to hit the belt with a stick a few times to knock it off the pulley wheel to disengage it from the wheel and so it would come to rest on the axle and there it would stay, resting lifeless and comatose until you needed that machine again when you had to reconnect the belt again. Doesn't sound much, does it? What I failed to mention was that this would be done whilst the pulleys were still moving. Hence, you had to be accurate with every strike of the stick. If you got the stick jammed between the pulley and the belt and didn't let go in time, it would throw you and the stick to the other side of the workshop.

I would stand and stare at the boss, a 70-year-old man who would be hitting this belt for all it was worth, like a madman hitting a snake up a rope, all this without taking his pipe from between his lips. He turned to me and shouted over the noise of the belts and machinery, 'You'll have to learn to do this in a couple of months' time.' You must be bloody joking; I won't be here in a couple of Months' I said under my breath.

In fact, I only lasted another three weeks before I'd had enough and handed in my notice. His parting words as he handed me my wages and P45 were, 'Whatever you do in life, don't' forget your time here and the great satisfaction that you can have working with wood.'

' Oh, I'm sure I won't,' I replied, remembering those close shaves I'd had with those killer pulleys and belts (no health and safety in those days.) 'Remember always to respect wood, because it will never answer you back.' I never, to this day, understood what he meant by that other that, in my opinion, he was as mad as a box of frogs.

Building the Dream

It wasn't too long before I secured employment again, and it happened to be in the building trade. This was brought about by some sound advice given to me by a bricklayer that I had known for some time. 'Do you know 'Tucks' cafe in Stroud?' I nodded in response. 'Well, if you sit in there on a Monday morning with nothing more than a cup of tea, you will get many builders popping in and looking for labourers who are available for work for a few days here and there.' I thanked him and made up my mind to give it a try after the weekend. Sure enough, by 9.30 am on Monday, I had secured myself a position with a local builder by the name of Tom Fudge. I was to labour for a couple of bricklayers for a couple of weeks. As it was wintertime, I would be finishing work at 4.30 pm, thus being able to get to my evening venues within a suitable time to fight, get home afterwards, a good night's sleep then up for work in the morning. What could possibly go wrong?

I was told that the mix was four shovels of sand and one of cement, put some water in first, then a bit of washing up liquid which keeps the mix pliable and easier to use, don't bang the shovel on the mixer drum as it will buckle it and stop it running true, don't let the mixer run out of diesel and above all keep the shovel out of the drum. Piece of cake, I thought to myself, so off I went.

Water in first then 1,2,3,4 of sand, 1 cement, more water and washing up liquid. It went nowhere in such a large drum, so I repeated it a few more times. Mmm... too stiff, more water. Bugger, it turned to soup.

Finally, I managed to get it right. Better just try a bit on the shovel to see if it looks right. That was the wrong move. The shovel got stuck in the barrel on one of the paddles that turns the mix. Up I went, over the top of the mixer and landed in the pile of sand face up. The two brickies looked over at the commotion, then at each other and without cracking a smile, one said to the other, 'I bet he won't do that again.'

Up On The Roof

It was a few labouring jobs later after ever more cups of tea in 'Tucks' cafe that I met a roofing contractor by the name of Mickey Chambers, and so began my next career as a roofer. There was only one slight drawback: I feared heights. 'That's no problem' said Mick,

'I'll soon cure you of that. Anyway, we'll be stripping off the old roof so your job will be loading the skips and generally picking up rubbish and keeping the site clear. Tomorrow the roofing materials will be arriving, and you can lend a hand with the unloading.' What he didn't tell me was that the lorries would not get down the narrow lane and would unload at the entrance of the driveway and that yours truly would spend the next three days with a wheelbarrow, moving everything nearer to the house.

Finally, payday came around as we all lined up to get our wages as in those days you were paid weekly by cash in a little brown pay packet. (Oh, happy days.) Mick turned to me and said 'oh, by the way, I've put your wages up on that chimney so if you want them, you'll have to go up and get them. I told you at the beginning that I would cure you of heights. Off you go then.'

It took me a good fifteen minutes to get there and back and as I arrived safely on god's earth, I called him all the names I could think of. Of course, he just laughed.

I got on well with Micky and his gang and stayed quite a long time. I even became quite a good roofer, which was a skill that I could use perhaps to get rid of the labourer's wages and get on to the tradesman's rate of pay. It never happened though as several other opportunities came my way.

Taking the Strain

Eventually, I found myself working for a large building company who built brand new houses, thirty at a time. It was a revelation. Portable loos, proper tool shed and a special Portakabin for our lunch breaks. There were several different trades on site at the same time and I found myself working with a small gang of pipe layers that I would be labouring to. They were a good bunch of lads, with the exception of Darren, who was an annoying sod. Darren was 16 years old and built like a brick one, and as daft as a brush. Often to be heard shouting his mouth off and stating that he was frightened of no one. That didn't include his mother, who was a formidable dragon in anyone's book. The lads didn't take any notice of his constant verbal and stupid ways but what they did find annoying was his constant habit of bumming food from everyone. He had eaten his food by lunchtime and would spend this precious hour of the day trying to scrounge anything that was edible. 'I'll have him,' said Tom the digger driver. 'Just wait until tomorrow. I'll teach him.'

The next day as lunchtime came around again, we were seated around chatting and eating when Tom piped up. 'Bloody hell, my missus has put a bar of chocolate in, and she knows I don't like chocolate.' 'I'll have it, I'll have it,' shouted Darren. We sat and watched as he devoured the whole bar. It wasn't until we arrived for work the next day that we were confronted with Darren's mother, and she was not in a good mood. 'Where is your sodding foreman?' she bellowed. We said nothing, but pointed to the Foreman's hut, just as he was coming out to give us our orders for the day. 'Can I help you Madam?' he said politely. 'You better bloody had' she shouted, 'who was the silly bugger that gave our Darren a bar of chocolate?' No one said a word.

'Well, it wasn't chocolate was it. No. It was a bar of bloody laxative, and what's more, when he was pushing his bike up that hill, he sh*t himself. I hope you are proud of yourselves, you irresponsible sods. It took hours to clean him up. He's in bed now, dehydrated and sweating like a pig. I'm taking this up with someone at the top. Who is your manager?'

The embarrassed foreman ushered her into his hut as he tried to calm her down. We were all asked in turn if we knew anything about it and of course, we didn't. I think someone mentioned that perhaps it was given to him on his way home.

I tried several different types of casual work during those early days but was always drawn back to the building trade. One of its main compensations was that for the rest of my life, I would be able to turn my hand to most things in the DIY field and over the years, have managed to save myself a lot of money.

The Garden

I had been working on the building sites to supplement my income as I hadn't been wrestling long enough in the early days to make a living at that time. However, when the bookings picked up and I was wrestling further afield, the building trade became difficult because I would have to leave earlier to get to the venues, which didn't go down too well with my employers. Some nights I would have to stay over and travel home the next day, so I became unreliable.

I had the idea that I would work for myself as I had become capable at things like fencing, laying patios, turfing and dry-stone walling. I decided to try my hand at landscape gardening. After a while the work began to take off and I could plan the work around my wrestling career and, of course, the money was better.

One day I was offered a small job for the local council and asked if I would care to put in a quotation. It was at a sheltered accommodation with a warden available day and night. The job was to take all the flower beds up and replace with turf for easier maintenance.

Seemed simple enough, so I went along to measure up for the turf. When I arrived there seemed to be no one there so I carried on measuring. In a few minutes, an old lady came up and in a booming voice, the sort of voice that can only come from a colonel's wife, 'What are you doing my good man?' I replied, 'I'm just measuring up for turf, all these beds are being put down to grass for easier maintenance.'

I bent down to continue when suddenly, I felt a crack across the back of my head. She had clouted a fourpenny one with a heavy metal garden trowel. It didn't quite knock me out, but I certainly saw stars. I sat there for a moment holding my head when I was aware that other people had arrived. I could hear talking but couldn't make sense of what was being said. I looked up and saw a lady looking down at me with a glass of water in her hand. I took the water and sipped at it.

'What the hell happened?' I mumbled. ' I'm Mary the warden and you have been set up on by Clara, she's an 87-year-old lady resident here.'

I was puzzled. 'Does she hit everyone who comes here?' She smiled and said, ' let's get you up and sit you on that bench, you will feel a bit better then.'

After a minute or two, I was beginning to think more clearly. The doctor had arrived, not for me, for the old girl. Apparently, she had worked herself up into a frenzy and needed some medication, and a police car had also arrived as someone must have called them.

'Why did she clock me one?' I asked the warden. 'She has been trying to stop this turfing from happening, she's a keen gardener and wanted her flower beds to stay. The council have been sending her some unpleasant letters about this and she probably thought it was you that sent them. when you turned up, she just lost it.'

Another lady brought me out a nice cup of tea and the warden went over to explain what had happened to the policemen. Eventually, the police came over to me. 'Good morning, sir, had a bit of a bump, have you?'

'Just a bit' I replied sarcastically. 'Do you know what' happened?' The first policeman said, 'we have got a statement from a gentleman who saw the whole thing from out of his window, it was him that sent for us.'

The other policeman spoke up. 'Do you want to press charges?'

'Of course I don't' I snapped at him, I'm a professional wrestler, this is just my day job, how is this going to look in the newspapers, 87-YEAR-OLD KOs WRESTLER. that's not going to do my career any good at all, I'd never live it down.'

'Oh, I see,' said the first policeman. 'So you re obviously used to a bit of violence then?'

He was beginning to get on my nerves. 'I am not violent,' I protested. 'I don't hit people, I fight other wrestlers in a bloody ring, and only when I get paid to do so.'

'I must apologize for my colleague,' said the second policeman. 'He meant no disrespect. So you don't want this taken any further? It's probably for the best, she would only plead provocation.'

'So I provoked her, did I? I'm the injured party here you know, have you spoken to her?'

'No sir,' came the reply, 'the doctor advised against it, they've put her to bed.'

'Okay, so I was only doing my job when this batty old woman assaulted me, she's gone to bed and I'm the one that's being questioned. Does that sound right to you? because it bloody well doesn't to me.'

'Well sir, I think that we can leave it there, we won't trouble you again.'

They got into their police car and left. I never finished the measuring because I had decided that I didn't want the job. If I had a smack in the head just for using a tape measure, what injuries was I likely to get using a shovel?

The Mixer

It was a while later when I was contracted to erect some fencing panels on an estate that was nearly completed. It was about 80 posts and panels, which meant a lot of holes to be dug, and posts concreted into place. The holes took ages to dig and it was a lot of hard work.

Then it was time for the concreting. The builders had left a pile of ballast along with a pile of sand. The problem was that the huge diesel mixer was near the pile of sand and the ballast, which I would be using was about 30 yards away which meant that I would have to move the mixer closer to the ballast. As I was the only one on site, it wasn't going to be easy.

I huffed and puffed and finally got the wheels free from the sand, and with a lot of effort it was on the move, very slowly. I soon became very impatient and took my eye off the ball and the next minute the mixer had fallen on its side with my leg trapped under it.

My vocabulary of bad language certainly improved over the next twenty minutes. I struggled to no avail to get that mixer off my leg until, fortunately, a chap came out of one of the nearby houses and came over to lend a hand. He managed to lift the barrel high enough for me to get my leg out. So far, so good.

As I tried to stand up, I felt a searing pain in my knee and couldn't move my leg. He suggested that he should drive me up to the hospital. Within about 30 minutes I was sitting in casualty. I thanked him and said that I could manage from here. So he left. It was about 3 hours later when I emerged from the hospital with a full cast on my leg and two crutches.

Luckily, I only lived ten minutes from the hospital and most of it was downhill. I set off taking it slowly, at least for the first few steps until I got my crutch stuck in a drain cover which took me a few minutes to get the bugger out then I was off again. I appeared to be getting the hang of it and went a bit faster... and faster and faster, until I had to run into a wall to stop. I reckon I had to do this about a dozen times until I reached home. By this time, not only did I have a bad leg, my right shoulder was killing me from the several clouts against the walls. I got into the house and collapsed into a chair.

Then it started – under the cast my leg was beginning to itch like mad. I used every instrument I could find to relieve the itching, but nothing would work. That was it, I'd had enough, I went down to the shed and with the aid of several tools, I cut the bloody cast off. Oh, the relief when I could have a damn good scratch, it was bliss. I searched around for a crepe bandage and a safety pin and wrapped up my knee. I pacified myself with the thought that it would still hurt whether it was in a cast or with a bandage, after all it wasn't broken, just tendon damage, a couple of days and it would be as right as rain. Of course, it wasn't, but at least I could drive again so I got a taxi to the housing estate and retrieved my vehicle.

The next day it was back to work, an d this time I had a couple of mates with me to help move that damn mixer. The three of us (well two and a half actually) managed to move the beast of a thing nearer to the ballast. The following morning saw me concreting the posts in. One of my mates came along to help me and we had it done in a couple of days. Now for the panels, that took us a further five days, but the job was a good one.

It was a further three weeks before I stepped back into the ring, and I took it easy for a while, Well, for the first round anyway. I must admit that I received serious reprimands from the hospital staff for taking the cast off but that was the least of my worries, what's another bo**ocking anyway?

A Right Royal Muck Up

I was helping my then brother-in-law to dig out some foundations for a building near where we lived in Stroud, Gloucestershire. It was just along the road to where the Duke and Duchess of Kent were in residence. On this day it had been raining and as he used his digger, one of the joints on the hydraulics had gone just as we were in the middle of the lane that led to the Royal household. There he was, cursing and swearing as he worked, up to his elbows in black grease. It was then that a Rolls Royce came up behind us. 'That's all I need' he muttered as he put down his spanner and headed for the car. He stood there for a minute as the chauffeur sat staring straight ahead, so he tapped on the window to advise him that he might want to go around to the next lane.

As he tapped on the window of this immaculately clean Roller, he noticed that he had left an oily fingerprint on the window. He panicked and quickly tried to wipe it off. That did it, the oil from his opened hand was smeared all over the window. 'Sod it!' he muttered. He shouted through the still closed window, apologizing and suggesting that they might want to go around as the digger was going nowhere for the next hour.

The rather snooty chauffeur was not amused, but the couple in the back started to smirk as they muttered something to the driver, who promptly turned around and drove off. I guess the rather snooty driver couldn't see the funny side of it but then I guess that he was the one who had to clean it off. It was a couple of hours later that we could finally set off again and do some work. I often have a chuckle to myself when I remember that day. I suppose that episode put paid to any chance of a knighthood.

The Scapegoat

In my persona as a gay boy, I would mince around the ring and try to break every rule in the book. Adorned with make-up, earrings, long blonde hair, sequined tights with glitter everywhere, I was hated by all who saw me. Of course, that was only in the ring (honestly).

One of my many antics was to pretend to give my opponents love bites. Of course, it never happened, but I was apprehensive as to how my opponents would react to it. Most knew me well enough not to be bothered by it, but the crowd would go mental. I never dreamt of the impact such actions would have on some wrestlers who had never met me before. No one was more surprised than I was when I started to get phone calls from wrestlers saying that if their girlfriends or wives saw a real love bite on their spouses' necks, would I tell them that I had done it in the ring the night before? I have often wondered how many relationships and marriages I had saved over the years. I know I had made a load of new friends that owed me.

Cars That Pass in the Night

I had been wrestling for a few years and found myself travelling further afield as I took on bookings from several promoters who put on shows all over the country. I felt it was time I got rid of my old banger and bought myself a more reliable car. A friend of mine who was a mechanic offered me a car that had belonged to his brother, who was selling it as he was emigrating to Australia. I popped around and had a good look at it. I noted the mileage and kicked the tyres, which was the extent of my mechanical knowledge. I felt I knew him well enough to be able to trust him, anyway, I knew where he lived.

The deal was done, cash exchanged hands and that was it, or so I thought. Talking to him over a cup of tea, he said rather sheepishly, 'there is one thing that I need to tell you. Whenever I passed my brother in this car, going the other way, we would always pass each other on the wrong side of the road.'

'How do you mean?' I asked.

'Well as we approached each other, I would go onto his side of the road and he would come on to my side, once we had passed, we would go back to our correct side. Of course, that was only if there were no other cars on the road at the time.' I looked at him somewhat bemused. 'Why?' 'I don't know' he said, 'it was just something that we did, so to be safe, I suggest we do the same, just in case I forget myself.'

I thought it was a strange request but decided to go along with it. Over the next couple of years, we must have performed that ritual a few dozen times. Then one day, he had forgotten to tell me that he had sold his car to an elderly neighbour. I will let you imagine the outcome. I will just say that a nasty situation was narrowly avoided. Just!!

You Never Know

To put on any wrestling show, there are many people that must come together to do various things that will make the evening a success. There are, of course, the promoters, the wrestlers, the seconds, referees, timekeepers, bill posters, ring riggers and many more. Out of all these people, I guess the ring riggers have the hardest job. Getting the ring to the venue is the easiest part. Depending on the facilities available, there are many times when this group of three or four strong men need to negotiate winding stairs and narrow passageways with large steel frames and corner posts, not to mention those heavy boards, along with hanging the lighting gantry high up in the ceiling above the ring.

Finally, when all this is completed, they must put out all the chairs ready for the audience to arrive. When the show was over, they would put everything back in its place and put the ring back on the van and away again. In those days they were not full time and would mainly be self-employed builders earning a bit extra to bump up their wages.

As a wrestler, I, like many others, started my career doing those jobs. They certainly earned our respect. In my fairground days on the wrestling booths, we had a couple of riggers that would help when we were in their area. In my case, it was the south-west. Imagine my surprise when a few years later I bumped into them again when I was working for the independent promoters. We travelled for a while together, often staying in the same digs and eating our meals and sharing our beers together. After all, this was the 70s and we had youth on our side. Good blokes I thought. That was until, many years later when I learned that one of them was Fred West, the notorious killer, known for burying his victims under his patio and in his cellar, aided by his then wife Rose.

Tag Team

A major part of being a wrestler is that sooner or later you are going to get involved in tag wrestling, which, for the uninitiated, consists of two wrestlers versus another twos. Popular in my day and as far as I know, still popular today. There are two ways to approach this – one way is to be paired up by the promoters and the other is to team up with another wrestler of your choice. In my case, it was preferable to choose the latter.

After much deliberating, I teamed up with a wrestler called Dennis. I had appeared a few times on the same bill as him in the past and although he had no persona of his own, he agreed to work the same one that I had adopted.

There was much discussion as to how this would work, but finally, we came up with an acceptable double persona. we would both appear to be gay, me with long blonde hair and him with jet black long hair. I wore white Lurex, and he wore black. Along with other differences, we appeared opposite in everything. Almost negative and positive, day and night, yin & yang as it were. It was a pleasing spectacle to lay before the public.

We seemed to be having success with this new pairing and gained a fair bit of work. However, two weeks later Dennis came up to me and said, 'This is not working out as well as I thought and it's causing me some concern.'

'How do you mean?' I replied. He came closer and sank his voice to a whisper. 'They think that I'm... er... one of them.' 'One of what?' I replied. 'You know. One of them gay boys.'

I looked at him and said, 'Well that's what they are supposed to think isn't it?'

'Well, I'm not happy about it.'

'I shouldn't worry about it' I said, 'They think I'm one as well and they have done for years, it makes me think I'm doing a bloody good job. Look, it's like this, when John Wayne is playing a cowboy, then for the duration of the film, he is that cowboy and people accept that, but when the film is over, he is just an actor.' 'Mmm, I suppose you're right.'

I'm not sure that he was convinced by my words, but he wandered off and spoke no more about it. I did however detect that his concerns about playing the gay boy were getting worse over the coming weeks and his performance in the ring was beginning to suffer, so it wasn't long before we finally put the lid on that partnership and The Sequins tag team was no more. I think he retired from the ring shortly after, and I heard no more of him for about ten years, when I happened to bump into a neighbour of his. 'Do you ever see Dennis at all?' I enquired. He said that he didn't and that he had moved away a few years previously. However, he had heard that he was living happily with his boyfriend, Stewart.

Oh, bloody hell, I thought, that was why he hadn't been happy in that persona. It never even crossed my mind. I don't think I'll ever take up psychology.

An Englishman, an Irishman and a Scotsman

There was an Englishman, an Irishman and a Scotsman in a bar. No, not really, but it was very similar.

When I was a young lad of about nineteen years old, I went through a stage when I could put away a good few beers in one session. Nothing remarkable about that you may think, but it took me about a year to realize that I couldn't take the hangovers and so I stuck to drinking tea. After all, I had come across plenty of drunken people on the fairground wrestling booth in my early days who would come out of a pub and thought that they were wrestlers so wanted to have a go at you in the ring, either to impress their mates or their girlfriends. You had to watch them as they could become dangerous to you or to themselves. Other than that, all you had to do is to amuse the crowds for the first two rounds and then spin them round twice and throw them into the corner post and let someone else clean up the mess.

I was wrestling somewhere near Birmingham. I don't remember the exact venue, but it was certainly in that area. The previous night I had been in Tewkesbury, so it was an easy trip to make and I arrived in plenty of time for that night's show. I was stood outside the hall signing a couple of autographs when a drunken local came out of the pub next door.

'Hey, you' he shouted, 'I want to see you.' Finally, he came over, having staggered a bit and one step forward and two steps back. 'You're a wrestler right.' I nodded. 'I think you're the one that put my sister up the duff.'

' I beg your pardon?' I retorted. 'She's pregnant' he shouted at the top of his voice. 'You got the wrong man mate,' I replied.

By this time, I was getting a bit annoyed with him. Every nerve ending in my body was telling me to punch him, but I don't do that sort of thing. Then one of the women came to my rescue. 'Just go home Peter, you're drunk. I know your sister and she's not bloody pregnant, you idiot.' He stood there swaying for a second then he turned to me and wagging his finger wildly in my direction said 'Ah well, she might have been and if she was, you might have been the father of her unborn child that she's not having.'

He sniffed sardonically, raised himself up to his full height and staggered off down the street. I turned to the woman. 'Is it just me or did I just miss the meaning of his last parting sentence?'

'No, it's just him. He's always like that after a skinfull,' she replied.

This next one happened in that lovely little seaside place of Weston-super-mare, a place where I had wrestled many times over the years. After the wrestling had finished and the crowd had dispersed, I wandered over the road to a little pub that I generally used to get a soft drink and a pie. The landlord would have a couple of posters in the pub and he knew to hold back a few pies for the wrestlers that went there after the shows. Although not a local, it was a place I would visit when in Weston and therefore I was on just a bit more than nodding terms with many locals.

I was chatting to a young couple who I had met on a previous visit when a drunken Scottish gent came bundling over. 'Here, I know you' he slurred.

'Do you?' I replied.

'Oh yes,' he said 'Give me a minute and I'll tell you who you are.'

'Okay, I'll wait then.'

I turned back to continue my conversation. It was a few minutes later when I felt a plucking at my sleeve and turned around. There he was again. 'I've got it, I know who you are now, do you want me to tell you who you are?'

'Go on then, surprise me' I said.

'You are Freddie Starr' he replied. He wandered off feeling smug, that his memory hadn't let him down.

I shook my head and turned back to my conversation only to see that the young couple were in fits of laughter. Ah well, I had made their night amusing anyway.

The third in this unfortunate trilogy took place in Liverpool. I had fought there on occasions but not often, so, I didn't know my way round. I needed a pair of bootlaces and asked a local man if he could point me in the direction of the nearest shoe shop.

As I wandered down the street, I was accosted by a drunken Irishman.

'Here, I know you' he said, 'you're a friend of mine.'

'I don't think so' I replied, 'I don't come from around here.'

'Oh yes you do, you are my friend. Now how would you like to buy a friend a drink.'

'No, you are mistaken,' I said.

Then the usual happened, and he started to turn nasty. 'You've always been the same, you think you're better than me because I have a drink now and then.'

'No honestly, I used to like a drink, there was a time that I was just like you.'

'What?' he said with his head on one side and totally flummoxed. 'You were Irish.'

I could do no more than sigh heavily and walk off, trying to think of a way to have answered him. I couldn't. I think it was William Shakespeare who penned that famous saying, 'There is nothing more daunting than being sober than when all about you are getting rat arsed. Ah well, maybe it was some other poet.

Vision in Lurex

It was in the early 70s that I took on my persona of a gay boy. Homosexuality (or at least the legality of it) was in its infancy and had become a subject of fun for many. I have in mind personalities such as Larry Grayson, John Inman and of course that great female impersonator, Danny La Rue, and I am bound to say that at the time, it did my ring career no harm at all.

I must also add that today, it has become a run of the mill thing and with it, has lost any stigma that was attached to it, quite rightly so in my opinion. I don't mind one little bit, just so long as the powers that be don't make it compulsory. In those early days, for me, it was not an easy ride, especially when it came to re-stocking my make-up box, because as with all people who wear silver sequined tights there came the inevitable ladders, snags and holes, so replacements had to be had on a regular basis.

I knew how it must have felt when the young lad stood in a chemist shop queue to buy condoms, hoping and praying that when it came to his turn, he would be served by the gentleman and not the young and usually gorgeous girl. The difference being if he came out with his preferred purchase or a tube of toothpaste.

It would bother me in the same way as buying silver tights. However, as time went by, that embarrassment disappeared, and life felt more comfortable. After all, I had made myself a laughing-stock within the ring, so I wasn't bothered outside.

On a day off I found myself in the centre of London and decided that I would spend the day wisely and give myself a long-awaited refurb. I entered a well-known store and made my way to the ladies' department, something I had done many times before.

It wasn't long before I made my choice, thanks to Mary Quant and took my purchases up to the very posh pay counter where I was met with a very posh assistant. I say she was posh; she looked like an air hostess on a night out. Very pleasant I thought, as she looked at my 5 packs of Lurex tights.

'Are you sure they are the right size for your good lady?' she said, 'they are the larger size.' Here we go, I thought, we'll have a bit of fun here.

'No. They are for me' I replied.

She looked at me for a moment and said, 'Is it for a fancy dress?' I looked her in a fake horror. 'They are for my work.' I waited for her to ask me what I did for a living and pitched in before she could frame such a question. ' I seem to go through a lot of these as the men I do business with are so rough.' She stood there, mouth wide open. Her colleague had obviously been listening to this conversation. I continued, 'I often think about packing it up but when I get my money at the end of the night then I feel a lot better about it. Still, we've all got to make a living. Can you direct me to the make-up department?' She pointed but said nothing.

'Thank you' I said and walked off. I would have loved to hear the conversation between her and her workmate. As I left, I turned and saw them in deep conversation.

Should I have come clean and told her of my real occupation and the need for me to make such a purchase? I thought not. With any luck, it could well have made their day and at the very least had given them something to relay to their families when they got home.

Pride Before A Fall

I was wrestling in one of the London suburbs, I can't remember the exact location but with an afternoon free, I took a leisurely stroll around the area with the idea of stopping somewhere for a lazy lunch.

Having time on my hands had become a rare commodity. You can imagine, the travelling in my job was time consuming to say the least.

It was a hot summer day, so it wasn't long before I was forced to find a bench in the shade. It was too early for lunch, so I bought a newspaper, found a suitable seat and read the paper.

It wasn't long before an elderly local couple came and sat beside me. 'Lovely day,' said the man. 'It's glorious' I replied, folding my newspaper, as it was apparent that he wanted to chat, and I didn't want to appear rude. 'I can tell by your accent that you are not from around here. Just visiting, eh?' he said.

My West Country accent had done it again, I thought. I explained my reason for my visit and as soon as I mentioned wrestling, that was it. Question after question came thick and fast. Did I know Mick McManus? What about Jackie Pallo? What was Les Kellet like? He clearly was a fan of wrestling and the more we talked, the more excited he got.

Apart from telling me how things have changed in his local area, how they had ruined it, all in the name of progress, the talk had been all about wrestling. After about 45 minutes, they got up to leave. He shook me by the hand, saying that he was pleased to have met me and I had made his day. They both wandered off up the road and as I watched them go, I felt pleased with myself that I had at least made his day.

I bet they don't get much company, I thought to myself as I crossed the road and went into a small café opposite. I sat at a table in the corner as the man came over with the menu. 'Was that you sat on the bench over there?' he asked. I said that it was. He continued,

'Do you know who you were talking to?' I must have looked rather vacant as he continued.

'That was Jack Haig.' I clearly had ignorance written all over my face 'Jack Haig, the comedy actor, played Monsieur Leclerc in Allo Allo. Also played in a couple of episodes of Dad's Army. He was offered the part of Corporal Jones but turned it down, so they gave the part to Clive Dunn. I thought that you were asking him about his career, you were talking for ages.'

I looked down in embarrassment. 'Yes, something like that,' I muttered. I ate my lunch in silence as I realized that the conceited side of me had certainly taken a good kicking that day and in my opinion, I thoroughly deserved it.

SENSE OF HUMOUR FAILURES

Like many people, i consider that I have a good sense of humour, as many will agree who read my first book. I guess it stems from my early days of watching those fantastic Carry On films and very often, I find myself quoting some of the funnier quips from them when a similar situation arises in my daily life.

One of my favourite quips came from that wonderful comedy actor Sir Norman Wisdom. Apparently, Norman was at a grand occasion held at Buckingham Palace. He was talking to the Duke of Edinburgh when there was a rather loud fanfare. 'What is that?' asked Norman, 'Her Majesty the Queen,' replied the Duke.

'She's bloody good on that trumpet,' said Norman. This is my humour and what a sad loss he is to the world. Another one that comes to mind is when some of the cast of Dad's Army were being interviewed. Clive Dunn came on blowing a bugle. Bill Pertwee said to him 'Clive, why are you blowing that bugle?' Clive said to him, 'Because it doesn't work if you suck it.'

Let me tell you some of my own quips but I must say they didn't all have that effect Whoops! One day, I found myself in the historic naval town of Portsmouth with a few hours to kill until I was due at that the wrestling venue. nearby What could I do for a few hours to amuse myself?

I had already done my washing for that week at a launderette in Havant, the day before. I considered my options and decided that it would be a trip to see HMS Victory. A bit of history would be a good thing for the soul I thought, so off I went to the naval dockyard.

For those of you who have never visited, I found it very impressive. There was about 30 of us waiting to board for the next tour available. Most were from Japan, a group of young girls on a hen weekend, a few couples and yours truly.

I have to say that I found it most instructive and interesting and somewhat entertaining, especially when the party of girls were climbing those very steep steps that you tend to get on such vessels, all wearing the miniskirts which were the fashion then. Well, I, forever the gentleman, let them go first of course The guide was doing a great job and eventually, we were on the top deck.

He pointed out the rigging, the crow's nest and the poop deck. 'Right then ladies & gentlemen' he said. 'If you would all like to turn around, you will see over there on the deck, a little wooden board and on it, a brass plaque. That is the very spot where Nelson fell.' It was no good.

I couldn't contain myself any longer. I spoke rather more loudly than I had meant to. 'I'm not surprised. I nearly tripped over the bloody thing myself.'

They all looked at me with blank faces. Our oriental bunch, not understanding, the girls just not getting it. The guide raised his eyes to the heavens and probably thought, oh no, not that old joke again. I kept my mouth shut for the rest of the tour.

The Dreaded Handbag

The poem that I penned at the start of *Confessions of a Wrestler* was inspired by the next item that I want to share with you. The only time that my own Mother came to see me wrestle was in a place called Stonehouse, not far from where I was born. She was an avid fan and attended many wrestling shows with the whole family, long before I took up the sport, so it was no big deal to her except that two of her sons were on the bill. My older brother Pete was a wrestler too until he started his own promotions. I was on first bout with a wrestler from Bristol called Terry Fear.

He was much bigger than me and so I had to rely on what I called my unforeseen advantage. Yes, you've guessed it, unforeseen by the ref but to my advantage. I managed to get to the third round and then Bang! Mother was up at the ringside, walloping me with her handbag and shouting, 'I never brought you up to behave like that!' This happened about three times until I finally got disqualified, which was not an unusual occurrence in my career.

There I was, 22 years old, getting a right pounding from a bigger bloke on one side and suffering a right-hand bagging from my own

Mum on the other. What a way to make a bloody living. The family rift lasted a couple of days but then settled down. For those who never saw the poem, I give it to you again.

The Lady In The Front Row

Why do you really hate me
As I strut around the ring
And start to hurl abuse at me
When I haven't done a thing?
I'm here to entertain you
And to win a bout or two
It doesn't help me, not one bit
When you spit and hiss and boo
You are such a dear old lady
Of that I have no doubt
But when I'm on the canvas
You treat me like a lout!
I'm just a harmless wrestler
Trying hard to earn a crust
You stub your fag out on my back
And try my head to bust
Take that brick out from your handbag
Sit back and take a rest
Enjoy the show for what it is
And let me do my best
We are both human beings
When all is said and done

After all, you are my mother
And I am still your son

Martin R Gillott

FROM SPANDEX TO HANDBAGS

Hilarious antics in the golden age of wrestling

This article was written by my good friend Wilf Archer and was first published for the Wrestlers' Reunion Scotland in their Reunion Programme for 2023. It refers to the previous article, the Dreaded Handbag.

Ah, the good old days of professional wrestling when men wore Spandex like it was a fashion statement and the crowd couldn't get enough of body slams and clothes lines. From the 1950s to the 1990s, the square circle was home to larger-than-life characters and unforgettable moments. So grab your folding chairs and prepare to take a trip down memory lane as we explore some amusing anecdotes from the glory days of old-style UK wrestling.

Picture this, a young wrestler, fresh-faced and eager to make a name for himself enters the ring with a twinkle in his eye and a mischievous plan in mind. He knows that the crowd wants a show, and he's ready to deliver. But little does he know that his capers are about to be outshone by a lady in the audience armed with a handbag and an unyielding sense of justice.

As our ambitious, youthful wrestler unleashes underhanded moves to rile up the crowd, this woman can no longer contain her frustration. She springs to her feet, handbag in hand, and charges towards the ring. The crowd's excitement reaches fever pitch as she rains blows upon the unsuspecting wrestler, who finds himself at the mercy of this unrelenting woman's wrath. During the chaos, with the crowd cheering on the handbag-wielding lady, our young wrestler manages to find his voice and cries out, 'Mum, for goodness sake, stop hitting me.' The audience erupts in laughter and applause, relishing in the unsuspecting turn of events. But it's the mother's response that truly steals the show. With a stern expression and thunder in her eyes, she looks her battered son in the eyes and delivers the line of the night: 'I brought you up to be better than this. Fight fairly because you are not too big to feel the weight of my slipper on your backside.'

The crowd, now completely won over by the comical scene unfolding before them, erupts into raucous laughter, appreciating the drama. In this uproarious tale, we see the clash of generations and the timeless values of fairness and sportsmanship. Even in the wide world of professional wrestling, a mother's love knows no bounds. It's a reminder that no matter how outrageous the stunts and storylines may be, there's always room for a good laugh and a touch of heartfelt mother's wisdom. So, my friends of the glory days of wrestling, we salute you. Your passion, loyalty and love of the sport have kept the flame alive through the years. Many have retired but at our reunion we get the opportunity to reflect on these hilarious and anecdotal moments.

So let us cherish the memories that make us laugh and remind us why we fell in love with professional wrestling in the first place. The next time you find yourself watching a wrestling match, remember the handbag and the words of a mother who expected her son to fight fairly. Because in the world of Spandex- clad heroes and larger-than-life personalities, it's the unexpected and humorous moments that truly stand the test of time. And hey, who knows, maybe one day we'll witness another wrestler armed with only a feather duster taking on a rowdy crowd. After all, in the wild world of professional wrestling, anything is still possible.

I cannot close without giving a special mention to Mr. Martin Gillott, aka Jackie Glitterboy Evans, the young, eager wrestler featured in the tale and his Mum.

Penned by the wrestler who used to stand in when one of the Harlequins Tag Team was ill or injured, he always looked grand, and the standard and the clever content were still seamless.

Whistle Stop Tour

One of the best things about working for many different promoters is that you get plenty of work. Okay, it means plenty of travelling from one venue to another, but it was worth it, except for the odd occasion when you had two on the same night which would mean first bout on, then a mad dash to the next venue to be last bout on.

We were called upon to do two bouts when we were working the Butlins camps as we did one show for the second lunch sitting then another show for the first lunch sitting, once they had finished. That was easy as it was the same venue. Imagine if the venues were 20 miles apart. Well, you know me, I had to go one better and do three in one day.

4 pm at a fete in Gloucester, then a quick dash to Weston-Super-Mare, on first bout, followed by an even quicker dash to Bath ready for the last bout. Having to travel with my make-up and sequins on, I was hoping and praying that I wouldn't get stopped by the police. That would have taken some explaining, as I didn't think that the early 70s were ready for that. It was bad enough when I had to stop

for petrol, I had some funny looks I can tell you, but then I didn't owe them any explanation.

Against all the odds, I managed to pull it off, but I vowed that I would never do that again. So stressful and of course, I had to drive home after. I slept well that night, I can tell you.

Showered With Embarrassment

I remember this evening well. It started off good. All wrestlers had arrived and there was a lively crowd out in the hall waiting to be entertained, the banter in the changing room was flowing and conversation was brisk. We were blessed with all the facilities
at this particular hall, so I put the kettle on and asked who wanted a cup of tea or coffee. 'I'll have a tea, two sugars' said Terry, one of the wrestlers.

Now don't get me wrong, he was a great guy, but he was a bugger when it came to practical jokes. Right, I thought to myself, see how you like this. I put two teaspoons of salt instead of sugar in his cup. 'Just stick it down there boy,' he said (he always called everyone boy). 'I'm trying to sort these laces out.' I left him to it as it was close to my bout and thought no more about it.

After the bout, I made my way back to the changing room and had a lovely hot shower. All was going well until I realized that someone had lifted all my clothes and my towel while I was in the shower. It was obvious who had done it. Now what could I do? I was stood there starkers and dripping wet when another wrestler came in.

'Hey Jackie, what's your kit doing out on that table? You'd better get it in before someone pinches it.' before I could do anything he had disappeared again.

Where is everyone I thought? Ah yes, it's the interval, they will all be up the bar and so will everybody else. If I just nipped out, grabbed my things and back in again no one will be the wiser, those that didn't drink will still be sat in the hall with any luck. Speaking of luck, it was certainly on my side that night. I managed to retrieve all my things without anyone seeing me. It did cause a lot of laughter among the lads in the changing room after the interval. However, I hadn't finished yet. I waited until he was safely in the ring then put all his clothes in the shower, turned the shower on, cold water of course, then left a pair of my Lurex sparkly tights and a note for him saying, 'To cover your modesty' I left the building. It was a good few months before I saw him again and to this day, as far as I know, it was never mentioned again.

Late On Parade

It was midwinter when I arrived at a venue in the suburbs of Birmingham after a nightmare of a trip. The weather was as wet as a duck's bum and the hall was a devil to find, with not many people out and about to ask the way.

However, I eventually arrived and made my way to the changing rooms, where I was pleasantly surprised to find that there was a roaring log fire, tea and coffee on tap and a table full of buffet food. I wish we had more venues like that – normally, we were lucky if they had warm water in the tap and a shower was a luxury. What's more, we had a television. Luxury indeed, so I made myself comfortable as I wasn't on until first bout after the interval. I put the television on. There were only four channels to choose from so I settled for Elvis Presley in a film called 'Girl Happy', or I think that's what it was called. My turn came around to enter the ring just as he started to sing 'Do not disturb' a song that I had never heard before, and I liked the sound of it.

I was stood there mesmerized by this new song when someone rushed into the changing room. 'Jackie, you're on! They are waiting for you.' I'll just hear the end of the song I thought, it won't hurt for them to wait a bit. It was nearly four minutes later when I heard the crowd getting impatient, stamping their feet and slow hand clapping. Oops, I thought, I'd better go now. I walked out to the ring among the boos and jeering from a slightly disgruntled crowd and entered the ring and shouted at them, 'Oh shut up, what's your problem? I'm worth waiting for.'

That did it. They went ballistic. I thought the promoter would have my guts for garters. I couldn't have been more wrong.

'What went on there then?' he asked at the end of the evening, after everyone had gone home. Before I could answer, he continued, 'The audience were a bit subdued tonight, I put it down to the crap weather, then you came in and whipped them up, they hated you before you started your bout. If you can do that every time, I'll see that you get more work from me.'

I stammered my thanks, accepted my wages and left. What happened there? I thought I was in for a right caning. He was true to his word and plied me with many further bookings, in fact, I probably worked more for him than any other promoter over the coming years. Yes, he was a good one to work for was Mr Duke Badger.

The Hen Party

It was in that lovely town Yeovil that we were wrestling one night. The bill looked good, and the crowd seemed lively. During the interval a couple of us who had already wrestled had got chatting to a couple of young ladies. It was quite clear that they were celebrating something, judging by the way they were dressed. It turned out that they were having a hen night, and we were talking to the bride to be and her chief bridesmaid.

Very soon, other members of their group joined them and asked us if we fancied going to their hen do, in the pub over the road, after the wrestling finished. 'Oh, I don't know' I said, 'the landlord might not like it, us lot crashing in.' 'It's okay' said the bride to be, ' the landlord is my dad.'

I said I would put it to the lads and let her know, one way or the other. I should have known better. Five of them jumped at it, so the six of us went over the road to join in the celebrations. What a shock we got when we saw that the pub was packed with the families of the bride, bridesmaids and a variety of friends from 18 years old up to about 70, men and women. It soon became apparent that this was no ordinary hen party. We chatted, laughed and joked with them all like we had known them forever. The music burst into life, the front door was locked, and the beer was on the house, it doesn't get much better than that.

Not being a drinker, I helped myself to a cup of tea that was on tap next to a lovely, laid out buffet and managed to find a comfy chair, where I sat and watched my mates getting slowly tipsy.

So relaxed was I that I started to nod off, only to be awaken by a loud voice over the loud music. 'Nein nein' it kept saying, 'nein nein.' I looked closer only to see Big Jimmy, (name changed of course) dancing with a lady who must have been well into her 70s. What's her husband making such a fuss about, I thought? Then I took a closer look and saw Big Jimmy giving her love bites. She was well up for it, but her German husband wasn't taking it so well.

It wasn't long before I suggested to the lads that I thought it was time that we took our leave. We said our thanks and goodbyes to our hosts, and we were let out of the locked door and into the street as I shouted back 'Somebody drag Big Jimmy out will you?'

Beware of the Bikers

This occurred one night in a show we were doing on the south coast. I don't remember the exact location, but it was in a Leisure Centre as they were called in those days, now they are known as Sports Centres.

Sitting in the changing room, chatting to the lads, the door flew open and in came Killer Ken Davies. 'It looks as though we have a capacity crowd in tonight' he uttered. I thought, great, that means the promoter won't ask us to take a cut in wages. Some of them did when it was a poor house. I'm sure I wasn't the only wrestler that had thought that either.

Ken came up to me and said, 'there are at least twenty leather clad bikers in the front row, they are going to love you, Glitterboy.' He chuckled. 'They'll bounce you around like a beachball.' I gulped. Oh shit, I thought, perhaps I had better curb my antics for tonight. But then the professional side of me kicked in. Why should I? the rest of the crowd had paid good money to see a good show and I couldn't let them down.

'What will be, will be' I said in the bravest voice I could muster and went to the loo for a nervous wee.

Later, as I was making my way to the ring, I did what I normally do. I stopped in front of the biggest of the leather clad gorillas and blew him a big kiss. What the hell did I do that for? I thought. His mouth opened into a big sneer and his eyebrows went up.

How I managed to get into that ring I'll never know. The bout lasted for six rounds when I was finally disqualified, which was not a rare occurrence in my case. By this time, most of the gorillas were up and banging on the side of the canvas shouting 'get him out, get him out'. I waited for the situation to calm down and they were all in their seats again before I left the ring, on the opposite side of course and made it back into the changing rooms unscathed.

Ken Davies, who had been watching the bout said, 'well you've got balls lad, I'll give you that.' I answered rather more quickly that I had meant to, 'I'll let you know when I've checked' followed by my best nervous laugh.

I quickly showered, dressed and removed my make-up, then went up to the bar to get my usual cup of tea whilst the main bout was underway. A while later when the wrestling had finished and so had my second cup of tea, a few stragglers were coming to the bar for a last drink and yes, you've guessed it, in came the bikers. Luckily, I was at the other end of the bar. They got their drinks and sat at a table near the door. I was toying with the idea of another cup of tea before I left when the biggest of the gorillas came over in my direction. Here we go, I thought, goodnight Vienna.

He came over, leant on the bar next to me, and stared at me with his face right up to mine. I must admit that my sphincter muscle was doing somersaults. I noticed a small monkey skull hanging from a chain from his jacket lapel and thought, I bet they visited the zoo on their way here tonight.

He said in a rather gruff voice, 'You and your mates have given us the best night's entertainment we've had in ages, and I'd like to buy you a drink.'

'Thanks, that's kind of you' I said, trying to discreetly hide my cup behind an empty beer glass. ' I'll have a pint of bitter please.'

He continued, 'Now come over and meet the lads.'

I must admit that they were all very pleasant to me and I answered all their wrestling questions amid what can only be described as biker talk, most of which went over my head, especially when they used words I'd never heard before such as Chapters and Prospects. 'Now then' said the head man, 'Would you mind autographing my helmet for me?' 'I beg your pardon?' I said with surprise. 'This one' he replied and put his motorbike helmet on the table. 'Oh er... yes of course.' Out came a permanent marker and I did as they requested to all the bikers' helmets.

After about half an hour, I took my leave. My parting words were 'good to meet you, and thanks for the drink. Another town, another dollar.' Did that sound biker enough? I thought so. As I approached the door, the biggest one shouted ' Hey Glitterboy!' I turned around and he blew me a big kiss. I could hear their laughter when they were halfway down the stairs.

The Ride of a Lifetime

Having fought and spent the night in Swindon, a young wrestler from the local area and I were due to appear on the same bill in Maidstone, in the lovely county of Kent. At the time I was without a car and took to taking a train. 'Why don't you travel down with me? He said. I thanked him and arranged to meet him in the car park opposite the guest house where I had stayed – it would be the quickest way and even if I gave him a couple of pounds petrol money, I would still be better off. The train wasn't that expensive but by the time I had got a taxi the other end, it worked out cheaper.

True to form, he arrived at the exact time stated and driving the biggest heap of junk I had seen on the road for a long time. He leapt out. 'You'll have to get in the driver's door and shuffle across as the passenger door is wired up and won't open. She's not much of a looker but at least she goes.'

I got in, with a bit of effort, he leapt in and slammed his door, and as he did, the passenger window fell into the inner workings of the door. 'Yea, that happens sometimes, I keep meaning to fix it,' he muttered. What the hell have I done? I thought. 'Did you get this car from a circus?' I asked. 'She's all right, just needs a little attention, that's all.' And off we went.

I settled down for the long and adventurous journey, and it wasn't long before I found out that every time he speeded up to change gear, my seat shot backwards by about six inches and when he slowed down it shot forward again.

He shouted to me over the sound of a very noisy engine, 'Make sure when you go backwards and forwards, you don't reeve up the mat, there's a slight hole in the floor which lets in the spray from the road.'

That's it, I said to myself, I'm not doing this a moment longer, I'm sitting in a death trap here. 'Look, just drop me at the next railway station, I'll feel safer taking the train.' '

'Nah, you'll be okay, she's a good little runner, don't worry, you can trust me, just sit back and relax.' Relax? He must be bloody joking. I could have hung on for dear life but the odds of whatever I hung on to comings away in my hands were too high for my liking.

We were driving up a hill at one point. Did I say driving? I meant crawling. As we neared the top at least a dozen cars were able to overtake as by then we were doing about five miles an hour. I said 'Shall I move the mat, put my feet through the hole and start running?'

'We're still moving aren't we?' he replied. We reached the top, thank goodness, and I thought, we've made it.

My troubles had only just begun. As we travelled down the next hill, we were getting faster and faster as we passed all the vehicles that had passed us on the way up. 'Hadn't you better apply the brakes?' 'No point' he said, 'they do work but sometimes you need to pump them to get them going.' 'If you keep driving like that, you're going to have to pump my chest to get me going, you bloody lunatic.'

I must say, against all odds and with a fair few prayers, we arrived at our destination. It took me a moment to get out due to the gearstick and my whole body shaking. 'We have made good time, shall we find somewhere and get a cup of tea?'

'TEA? You must be bloody joking, I need a brandy.'

'I thought you didn't drink' he said.

'I didn't, until I accepted a lift in your bloody heap.'

It wasn't the best bout I ever had that night, but I managed to pull it off. Afterwards, in the bar he came up to me. 'Do you want a lift back?' he asked.

'Where are you going?'

'Back to Swindon'

'Ah, no thanks, I'm off to Glasgow, I've got a taxi booked to take me to the train station.'

I was going to Stroud, just the other side of Swindon, but I certainly wasn't travelling with him ever again.

Holding a Grudge

There are a few wrestling fans that think that because we wrestlers fight each other, we hate each other. This could not be further from the truth. In the main, we have respect for each other and personally speaking, have good mates in the business.

However, there are exceptions to this. Like any other walks of life, there are those who, for a variety of reasons, hate each other. You must realize that most wrestlers have a certain amount of attitude, after all, we wouldn't have entered the business without a certain amount of it running through our veins.

It was a promoter's nightmare as some wouldn't appear on the same bill as their arch enemies. It could have been a ticking time bomb in some of the worst cases. Luckily, I didn't come across this many times in my own career but listening to others, it happened more often than I had originally thought. Fortunately, it only happened to me on one occasion, and I dealt with that story in my first book and do not wish to visit it again. Some last a couple of nights and others can last over years and years. As you can imagine if they did get in the ring together it usually would end in bloodshed and permanent physical damage, so that was avoided at all costs.

It's not a subject that I, or most wrestlers, wish to talk about. However, I feel that I would be failing in my duty if I made no mention of it. I believe that you, the reader, has a right to know the facts about wrestling.

Music to my Ears

It wasn't always for me to choose what days off I would give myself. That was generally down to the promoters and when they wanted me. By this time, I was working for many promoters so I would be needed as and when the call came. If I managed to get a day off, there was nothing better than to take it when I was in shouting distance of Oxford. This bit of old England, as well of being rich in architecture, is also a leading light in the matter of education, knowledge and learning. It boasts many colleges, museums and libraries within this city known as the 'Dreaming Spires'. Whenever I had the chance, I found there was nothing better than listening to the music of the street entertainers of that lovely city, who were clearly students at the nearby college of music, eking out their meagre student grants. If when walking past I was greeted by the sound of three of them on their violins, I would immediately take a seat at the nearest table of an outside café, order a pot of tea and let the music do its magic.

I remember one day when they were joined by a young girl pulling a harp on a trolley, setting it up and playing along. Then a young man with a double bass would also join in, followed by two flautists. Between them all, they would create a wonderful sound and would play on whilst their open violin case attracted coins and notes of all denominations from passers by, and yes, I made many contributions to that worthy cause.

I must have spent many hours over the years and indeed, not a small amount of money, but always felt that it was money well spent for the hours of relaxation and entertainment that I received in exchange. Without sounding too poetical, I viewed it as a little bit of heaven on earth and have often thought about it over the years.

Who's A Pretty Boy Then?

It must have been in the mid 70s on yet another trip to Wales, working for one of my best promoters, Mr. Evan Trehearne. Evan was the top man behind the well-known wrestling magazine of the day 'The Ring Sport', covering wrestling and boxing information of the day, and a great promoter in Wales.

I remember it well as we spent quite a long time trying to get digs for the night. There must have been something big happening on the same night because all out usual haunts were fully booked. However, one of the lads came across a farmhouse which was willing to take the five of us in. We were sure of a good breakfast in the morning, but there was a snag - there was only one room for all of us. There was a double bed, and they would put up another three beds whilst we were out at the wrestling. Better than nothing we thought, so we agreed.

At the end of the evening, the five of us wended our way back to the farm and were welcomed with a tray of hot chocolate, which went down a treat. We chatted to our hosts until our eyes started to droop, then off to bed we went, after drawing straws to see who would sleep in the bed. I drew one of the short straws so was consigned to a camp bed.

When we got to the room, we found it a bit of a tight squeeze. The makeshift bedroom had obviously been furnished as a bed it with furniture taking up a lot of the floor, and hanging from a chain in the ceiling was a parrot in a cage

I managed to sleep quite well except when Mickey (name changed) started to snore and did so on and off for the rest of the night. When we awoke the next morning, he was the last one awake. The rest of us were sat talking when he suddenly awoke with an awful coughing fit. 'Are you all right mate?' He couldn't answer for coughing. Eventually, we found that whilst he had been sleeping, the bloody parrot had been flicking bits from the bottom of his cage straight into Mickey's open mouth. Serves him right for snoring.

The Maverick

Occasionally, someone appears on the wrestling scene who turns out to be a right pain in the butt, and the highest contender in this category had to be the would-be wrestler who went under the name of The Maverick. He had clearly done the rounds of all the promoters looking for work, but nobody wanted to use him. Why was that, you ask? Simple, he couldn't wrestle. Clearly, he had not trained with any wrestling gym but through watching it on the television, he had convinced himself that he was fantastic and could do what they had done with no experience at all. He thought his way into the business was to turn up at the halls on the night of a wrestling show, disappear into the toilets and come out dressed in his wrestling gear, rush to the front of the ring, jump up on the apron and challenge the wrestlers to a fight, only to be thrown out by the management.

I had seen him try this a few times in the past, always with the same result, but clearly, he wasn't going to give up. That is until one well-known promoter was heard to say, 'I've had enough of this joker, it's time he was taught a lesson.' The promoter took him to one side and said, 'Okay son you've made your point, I'll give you a bout at the show next month.' The man jumped at it, telling the promoter that he wouldn't regret it, and left. I heard the promoter mumble 'No, but you will mate.'

I wasn't present at the next show, but I got the low down from a couple of the other lads that were. The promoter was true to his word and put him in the ring with none other than Killer Ken Davies. Remember me telling you earlier in this book how Killer Ken was the hardest wrestler I had ever worked with? Mine was only 3x3 minute rounds. This was to be 8x5 minute rounds.

A lamb to the slaughter, to be fair, and having known Ken for many years by then, he just did his normal wrestling moves and with the usual power that he always used, no more, no less. By the start of the second round, the maverick was crying to get out of the ring, but

Ken kept him in until the end of the second round, when a body slam just about finished him off. What made it worse was that a lot of the maverick's friends had come to see him annihilate his opponent.

The first thing that Ken said when he left the ring was 'I did nothing to him that I wouldn't have done to any opponent.' The Maverick was never seen around the halls again to my knowledge.

Violent Wrestlers

I remember many years ago being asked by a member of the Women's Institute as I gave them a talk, 'Were you born into a household of violence, or did you become violent later on in life?' I thought to myself, what sort of a question is that to ask?

I think I may have mentioned this in my previous book, but it just goes to prove that some people have the wrong concept of wrestlers and think they are steeped in malevolence and physical mayhem. This is so far from the truth that it is almost laughable.

I was in the business and don't think I have ever met or even heard of a wrestler with those traits. Do these people think all professional footballers go around kicking people to death? Of course not. Take it from me, your average wrestler plies his trade to make ends meet for his family. They have even been known to invite their mothers-in-law round for Sunday lunch. Some go to church, and I know at least one that regularly read the sermon. One wrestler was even a fully-fledged vicar. How much more proof do they need? Wrestlers are not, and never were thugs. And anyone who says we were is going to get a right slapping (only joking).

Keeping Fit

This little episode happened about two years after I hung up my boots for the last time. I say the last time, but I did manage to squeeze in one more bout, at Butlins holiday camp in Minehead. I was there enjoying a well-deserved holiday when I happened to bump into a wrestler that I had worked with many times in my early career and who was now the promoter in that venue. He was telling me that one of the wrestlers on the bill had failed to turn up and if he could provide me with boots, trunks etc. would I stand in, and I, of course obliged.

I had been out of the game for about six months by then and didn't it show. I was like a sack of potatoes being thrown around the ring. I lasted three rounds before I left the ring; I was totally knackered.

A few years passed before my lack of fitness once again raised its ugly head. I happened to be walking through my local town of Andover when I caught sight of a little fat bloke in a shop window. Who's that? I thought, then it dawned on me that it was my reflection in the window. I was shocked. That's it I thought, as from tomorrow, things are going to change, I'm not looking in any more shop windows.

I had to do something about this onset of obesity. I needed to give it some serious thought, so I went into a coffee shop to buy a drink and think seriously as to what I needed to do. I was queuing for my drink, deep in thought whilst gazing into space when a rotund lady shouted at me in a rather unsavoury tone, 'Are you looking at me?' I turned round abruptly and replied, 'I'm so sorry madam, I was just thinking how attractive you are 'Oh thank you' she replied, rather coyly, 'I'm stuck for words.' I thought to myself, and so you should be you ugly, gobby cow.

My drink now purchased, and a seat found, I began to think about my obesity dilemma. I didn't want to join a gym as I had already been down that route and gyms had changed so much since my day, from temples of fitness to roomfuls of posers and wannabe strong men with young giggly girls in leotards.

Then it suddenly came to me. Every Monday and Thursday night, I took my daughter Donna to Tae Kwon-Do. I could do a lot worse than join them. It was either that or Tai Chi and as I didn't relish going down the route of directing imaginary traffic in the park, Tae Kwon-Do it was then.

Within a couple of months, I had purchased all the gear that I needed and had taken up my place in the ranks, at the back of the hall with the beginners. I gradually worked my way up to my first grading. We had taken over a large village hall near Winchester for the day. The grading was going well and as a beginner, I was up first and was finished by eleven thirty. We still had to wait all day as there was a talk from the head examiner at the end which we were compelled to attend in full uniform.

It was lunchtime when we devoured our sandwiches, brought from home, while tea and coffee were supplied by the management. A few of us went outside for a cigarette, which we were allowed to do providing we took our belts off. When the thirty-minute lunch break was over, we were all called back inside to continue the grading. Without thinking, I took my last puff, chucked my cigarette butt down and scuffed it out with my foot. A second later I realized I had stubbed it out with no shoes or socks on. A pain and a moment I will never forget.

A few months later, around Christmas time, like many clubs, a Christmas bash was organized at a night club in nearby Chippenham. A couple of days before, we were all taken aside and told that this night of enjoyment would see several local Tae Kwon-Do clubs gathering to celebrate the festive season and there would be several black belts on the doors making sure that there would be no trouble. Any trouble would result in those involved losing their Tae Kwon-Do licences.

This made for a very enjoyable evening and for me, who had never liked night clubs and avoided them at every opportunity, it was quite a mean feat. I have always felt that apart from the loud music, it was like watching a firework display whilst sitting in a coal scuttle. The other thing that amused me was when some bloke upset his drink over someone else. The conversation went like this.

'Oh, sorry mate, it was an accident.'

'That's okay, I can see you didn't mean it. Let me get you another drink.'

'No, it's okay, let me get you one.' And so on. Normally, in a night club, this would have ended in fisticuffs, but because of the threat of losing your licence, it was more like a Two Ronnies sketch. The evening went without a hitch.

It felt weird though. As we all shook hands with the bouncers, we thanked them for a wonderful evening and wished them the compliments of the season as we left. I continued with Tae Kwon-Do for a few years but with the feeling that I had taken it as far as I wanted to. I left a fitter and I hope, a wiser person.

Hello Again Grapple Fans

For 33 years, this man was virtually on our screens every week and whilst his face was rarely ever shown he had a voice that was known to millions. We are of course talking about the man who was known as 'the voice of wrestling' – Kent Walton. It doesn't seem right to write about wrestling without giving this man a mention.

He was born on August 22nd 1917 in Cairo, but the family moved to Surrey when Kent was still a young boy. Initially he pursued an acting career, enrolling at the Embassy School of Acting in London, but the outbreak of World War 2 put a stop to this promising career as he served his country as a radio operator and front gunner.

Returning to the UK after the war he resumed his acting career, but thanks to his dulcet tones, he was offered a job as a sports commentator and asked to cover football league matches and tennis at Wimbledon. On the 9th of November 1955, Kent commentated on his first wrestling show for ITV.

Initially he had no knowledge or indeed interest in the sport and basically had to: learn on the job, ably assisted by Mick McManus and Mike Marino. However, despite his rocky start to his wrestling commentating career, he would remain a fixture on the wrestling scene until it was cancelled in 1988, a remarkable and unparalleled 33 continuous years. It was often said that he and he alone could make a wrestler a star, be loved or be hated just by what he said about them in his commentary. He also had his own catchphrases: 'Greetings grapple fans' and 'Have a good week until next week', which became legendary, and of course not one single masked wrestler in 33 years would ever talk to him in the dressing room.

As well as being the beloved commentator on World of Sport, Kent would combine this with other successes including fronting the first pop show on television, 'Cool for Cats' and was also a radio disc jockey. He made many other television appearances, providing the voices to countless television commercials over the years.

When wrestling ended in 1988 Kent left ITV Sport. However, in 1991 Grampian TV filmed several shows to be broadcast in their region and he agreed to provide the commentary. He did not attend the venues and commentate 'live' – instead this was put on some days later with the commentary recorded in a London studio.

Away from wrestling, he owned and ran a very successful film production company. Kent always remained fond of wrestling and was a staunch supporter of the Wrestlers' Reunion, and in its early days he would attend the events at both Joe Cornelius and Wayne Bridge's pubs. Kent is only one of three non-wrestlers to be inducted into the British Wrestlers Hall of Fame

Kent died on the 24th of August 2003 aged 86. He was a true pioneer and legend in the wrestling industry. Credit should be given to him for not only his commentary duties but also for building the careers of many of the top stars in the business.

The Day the Ring Broke Down

I remember this incident well; it happened one Tuesday night in Yate, near Bristol. Everything was going smoothly, the first bout had gone well and ended in a draw, both wrestlers gave it their all and displayed some excellent moves and counter moves to the delight of an appreciative audience.

Then it was my turn to fight before the interval. I was on with a local wrestler named Terry Fear. We had fought each other a few times before so there would be no surprises as we had the measure of each other.

It was the usual eight rounds of five minutes each round. Things were going well until the start of round six, when I was thrown the length of the ring. The crowd was cheering because I was getting my comeuppance for fighting dirty in the previous rounds. Suddenly, there was a tremendous crack from underneath the ring and the whole structure lurched to one side.

We did the best we could and carried on while the promoter got under the ring to see what the trouble was. He wasn't best pleased when we came out, but we carried on. Apparently, a weld had broken on one of the metal struts the middle one of five.

At the end of the round the Master of Ceremonies entered the ring and made an announcement. 'Ladies and gentlemen, is there a welder in the house?' I couldn't see what was happening, but a chap came forward and was talking to the promoter.

We finished our bout in round eight as I was finally disqualified (yet again). As the interval started, all wrestlers were summoned to the ring while most of the crowd had retired to the bar. We took off the apron on one side of the ring, pulled the canvas back to just over halfway, lifted the padding and removed the centre board. The emergency welder climbed under the ring with his equipment and promptly made a repair on the damaged strut. After about ten minutes when the weld had cooled down, we quickly re-assembled the ring ready for the third bout. The ring lasted well throughout the remaining two bouts when the ring was packed up and put in the van.

I retired to the bar for a quick drink and got talking to the welder. 'I hope he put his hand in his pocket and saw you right' I said. 'Oh he put his hand in his pocket and left the bugger there. He gave me a free ticket for the raffle.' Tight sod, I thought, because the bottle of brandy for the raffle was the same one he raffled night after night and funnily enough, his wife won it most times, either that or a wrestler won it and had to give it back at the end of the night. I couldn't tell him that, could I?

'I'll tell you what, I'll give you his name and address, you can send him a bill,' I said. 'That's fair' he said, 'I'll do that.' I added, 'but it never came from me, right?'

I don't know if he did this and whether he got paid, I hope so. Nothing was ever mentioned about it, and I never asked. I did hear that he gave the ring a complete overhaul and tested every weld, and all the boards were tested and repaired where needed. One good thing came out of it. I did hear that someone nicked his bottle of brandy from his vehicle a few nights later.

Keeping Up The Persona

One question that comes up now and again from some interested parties is, how do you manage to keep up your persona so that it remains believable? My persona had been honed over a period of a couple of months before I laid it in front of an audience.

I started by studying people that were gay or appeared to be gay – it was not easy to tell in those days. Nowadays they leave you in no doubt with their flamboyant ways in dress code, their mannerisms, the way they talk. Now they shout it from the rooftops, but it wasn't like that in my day.

I met many as I was perfecting my persona and all of them thought it was fascinating what I was doing with it. I also spoke to many ladies and took on board any make-up tips that they passed on to me. Once I was up and running (well, mincing) I discovered that it wasn't enough to confine my persona to the ring, I was going to have to continue from the time I entered the venue until the time I left the building, sometimes longer if we went to a nearby bar after the show or for a meal in the local area. As you may already know, I played a heel (villain) as that suited my persona. I never smiled or laughed as that would have given it away.

Having said that, there were a few times when I got caught out. One time I remember was one night in Cardiff. I was having a particularly difficult bout as the person I was fighting took no prisoners. He turned me around, lifted me up, threw me on the canvas and spun me around, first by one leg then by both. I'm sure the audience thought we were Torville and Dean and not two hairy-arsed wrestlers.

Finally, he threw me from one side of the ring to the other. I kept on going through the bottom rope and landed on my feet, but the momentum meant that I fell forwards and landed headfirst between the legs of an elderly lady in the front row.

She turned to her friend and shouted, ' Do you know Shirley, that's the first time I've had a man between my legs in fifty years, and it had to be a gay bloke.' The audience erupted in laughter. As I got to my feet, I also saw the funny side and started to laugh at her comment.

That was it, the crowd didn't take me seriously from that time on. Whenever I was thrown someone would make a comical quip. I had lost my audience and throughout the rest of the bout, I never got them back. Serves me right for laughing

A Change of Career

Many wrestlers, when they retire from the ring, take up another career. A lot of them take pubs and eke out their working lives as genial landlords and of course, landladies. I think I mentioned this in my last book. At the risk of repeating myself, I will mention it again. We all knew that the golden era of wrestling was coming to an end as far as the television wrestling was concerned.

I was sat in a service station late one night, returning from a show, with two of my wrestling buddies, Big Pat 'Bomber' Roach and Brian Glover, who wrestled as Leon Arras. The discussion soon came up as to what we would do. We all knew that once wrestling was taken off the television, it would spend the end of our careers as we knew it. Both Pat and Brian had carved themselves out successful careers in acting so that would be their natural choice and as it happened, looking back, two great choices, as we all know.

Would I try to do the same? I didn't think so. I quite fancied doing it on an amateur basis and maybe the odd bit of extra work or walk on parts but I wouldn't try and make a living at it. I told them of my plans to become an osteopath or a physio, after all, I had spent the last few years bending muscles and bones about, so it was probably time that I tried to repair a few. How did my new career work out? Read on.

My first step was to pass a massage course. I duly signed up with the Northern Institute of Massage based in Blackpool, mainly to see if this line of work would suit me and indeed, if I suited this line of work. If it worked out then I knew it would be worth pursuing and sign up for a more extensive and indeed, more expensive business, like osteopathy or something similar. My first course was under a tutor named Ken Woodward who later in years handed over the reins to my good friend and great wrestler Edwin Caldwell, who wrestled under the name of Eddie Rose. A magnificent wrestler and a great Author of a couple of very interesting wrestling books. What a small world.

I ended up taking over a dozen different courses to end up where I wanted to be and with good results in my exams. Was it easy? No, it wasn't. First, I assumed that my years of wrestling experience had taught me a lot about muscles, bones and general injuries. How wrong was I. It very quickly became apparent that what I knew was nothing compared to what I needed to know.

An old school friend I met up with many years later said to me 'How come you did a lot better than me when we both had the same start in life?' 'Simple' I replied, 'When you were in the pub getting rat arsed with all your mates, I was burning the midnight oil with my nose stuck into books for hours on end. It wasn't easy. Nothing worth having in life is easy.'

As I had started my new career later in life, it all had to be paid for. Coupled with the fact that I had a wife and baby daughter to support, I needed an income. This took the form of going into service, where I became a gardener/handyman, chauffeur, butler and general dogsbody whilst my wife did the cleaning, cooking etc. My main hours were from 6 am until 2 pm with the occasional stint as butler/waiter for dinner parties.

The rest of my waking hours would be swallowed up with studying and trips to college and eventually, university, when I had to make up my hours over the weekends. This went on for about three years, when I was invited to join an established practice in my local High Street. I somehow managed to buy a small house nearby and left the employ of the service industry, working mainly in the massage department, but it was a start, and I worked alongside osteopaths, physios, beauty therapists and a chiropodist. Working in this environment opened doors that I could benefit from with the remaining four years of study in front of me.

THE NAKED TRUTH

You can't be in any walk of life without it throwing up some humorous moments. I will now share some of these with you. Obviously abiding by the rules of professional ethics, I will not be including any names of patients.

The first event happened within a few weeks of entering my first practice. The lady in question had clearly never had massage before, so I went through the usual preliminaries, any allergies etc. Then I explained about lying face down and placing the towel over her blah blah.

I left the treatment room saying that I would be back in a few minutes and I would knock on the door to make sure that she was decent. Then I went to reception to wait for what I thought was a respectable time. A minute later, she appeared in reception naked, holding up the towel and said, ' I can't remember what you said to do with the towel.' I have never moved so fast in my life, grabbing the towel, putting it around her and bundling her back into the room.

I was truly glad that it was the chiropodist's day off, otherwise we would have had a waiting room full of pensioners and you could bet that at least two of them would have had pacemakers.

Some Sort of Idiot

It has always been my policy to do home visits when necessary. After all, some people with certain physical injuries are unable to get out of bed, let alone to travel to the surgery. For those unfortunate patients, I would always arrange to visit them, usually after my surgery was completed for the day. On this home visit to a new patient, armed with my little bag of tricks and the gentleman's address, I drove to his house. As I pulled up outside, I realized I hadn't written down his name. I thought to myself, come on think, what was his name? Then I remembered that Pratt was the name of the person who was looking after him. I knocked and he came to the door. 'Hello Mr Pratt, I'm here to see the patient.'

'He's upstairs, first door on the left, my name is not Pratt, It's Burke.' I apologized but thought to myself, well I knew it was some sort of idiot. Sometimes, it's difficult to keep a straight face in those circumstances. However, I don't think he was in a laughing mood.

Washday

Another home visit that sticks in my mind was when I was called out to an elderly lady who had damaged her back whilst doing her weekly washing. It was her son who contacted me, and he lived many miles away. I managed to find the house with just a little difficulty, and knocked on the door. A voice shouted 'Around the back' so around I went. I was confronted with the lady of the house holding for dear life onto the washing line, letting out a scream every time the wind blew and moved the washing that was already on the line. Her unconcerned husband was leaning on the fence with his back to her, smoking his pipe.

I tried and tried many times to get her to lean on me and to let go of the line, but still she clung on. After about half an hour, I managed to get her to let go with one hand. It was a start, but I still had to get her to let go altogether so that I could get her up the path and into the house. 'Are you going to be much longer?' said her husband, 'only it's nearly dinner time.

'I'm doing what I can,' I said in an offhand manner. 'Have you got a better way then?' I asked, rather more sarcastically than I had meant to. He took his pipe out of his mouth and after giving me a hard stare he replied. 'Yes. Why don't you just put the bloody prop up and leave her. She'll come in when it rains.'

I did eventually get her inside and comfortable. I did what needed doing and with a couple of days taking it easy, she was back to normal. I still don't know if her old man got his dinner.

The Raffle

It doesn't matter what trade or profession you enter in to, sooner or later, someone may call upon your knowledge and time and invite you to come along to their club and give a talk or to demonstrate your chosen subject for their entertainment. I have been called on many occasions to ply my trade at a variety of institutes. Some of them were enjoyable whilst others turned out to be hard work and on the odd occasion, a total waste of time. A few give you your expenses whilst the majority offer you a cup of tea.

The one that I want to share with you now comes because of one of my many hobbies. For many years now, I have taken great pleasure in oil painting, with various degrees of success. A few have been sold, many have been given away and even more have been scrapped.

It was my mother-in-law who that persuaded me to go along to her Monday Club and do them a landscape in oil in exchange for a roast dinner and copious amounts of tea. On arrival I set up my equipment, in between being introduced to everyone individually by a somewhat gloating ma-in-law, who enjoyed every minute of being in the limelight. As I was presented with my first of many cuppas, she had a word in my ear. 'Whatever you do, don't buy a raffle ticket.'

'Why not?' I enquired. She proceeded to tell me that the Members bring along one raffle prize each week, a tin of beans etc, then they are allowed to buy one raffle ticket each. This way, everybody wins a prize, so If I bought a ticket, someone wouldn't get one. It took a while to figure out what she meant but then I saw the funny side of it and couldn't stop laughing.

'This is serious stuff,' she said, and I just knew she meant it. I considered myself firmly put in my place. The painting demonstration went down well, and I was asked back a couple more times. I think that those who stayed awake long enough really enjoyed it.

Johnny Johnson

Whilst writing the last tale, I was reminded of a friend of mine a few years ago, so I will share this one with you as well. Johnny Johnson was a bit of a singer during the last years of the Second World War. He even went on to appear in Lionel Bart's musical The Blitz. He had been a competent singer, although in his later years, he was better described as a passable drunken karaoke singer. Nevertheless, he was quite popular on the local old people's homes.

I bumped into him in town one day and asked him if he was still doing the rounds. To my dismay, he gave a big sigh and said that he had not been needed lately and that the last one he had done went less than well. Apparently, he only had an audience of seven. Six had fallen asleep about halfway through and the other one had died. Well, he was 97 years old. I'm sure the devil was with me when I burst into uncontrollable laughter. He hasn't spoke to me since.

Treading the Boards

Along with this new career, I now had the time to pursue other interests I had thought about over the years and one of those was amateur dramatics. I well remembered a few years previously that conversation between a couple of wrestling mates about what we would do as a next career. Both decided to go into professional drama whilst I wasn't going to give up the day job, as the old saying goes. They had both met with great success in that industry, so I decided to try my hand in the amateur sector.

So, one dark winter's night, I found myself going along to a local group called the Prior's Players who were meeting to read through a play called *Blithe Spirit* by that great playwright Noel Coward. I was made most welcome by the other members and asked what part I would like to audition for. 'I'm quite happy helping behind stage' I said nervously, 'in fact I might as well tell you now that you will never get me on that stage.' True to my word, they never did...well, not for the first few months anyway. It wasn't long before they cajoled me into doing a small walk-on bit in an old-time music hall and the odd pantomime. It took them a full year before they were able to put a script in my hand and say, 'you're playing the lead part.'

I was to play the part of Billy in that popular stage play of the day *Billy Liar*. Oh my god, I thought as I flipped through the script, look at all those lines I need to learn.

The night of the first show came far too quickly and as I stood in the wings waiting for the opening music, one of the stagehands came up to me and whispered in my ear, 'You're nervous aren't you' 'You have no idea,' I whispered back. 'Here, take one of these.' he offered me a pill. 'Mild tranquilizer' he said. My tongue came out like a bloody chameleon and the pill went down faster than a lady of the night's knickers.

'Do they work?' I enquired. 'They worked great for our dog on long car journeys' he replied, 'She wasn't sick once.' 'Well, if I start cocking my leg against the furniture, it's your fault', I hissed with more venom than was called for.

How I got through to the interval I do not know. My nerves were clanging like a town crier's bell. Then came the second round. Oops sorry, forgot myself, the second act. Again, I was waiting in the wings when the oldest and wisest member of the cast, who was playing my father, spoke. 'Well, we re-wrote the first act, now let's see what we can do with the bloody second.' We all chuckled as quietly as we dared and from that moment on, I felt the nerves slowly disappear.

All in all, it turned out well and the audience never suspected the mistakes, which was something of a miracle. After all, we had buried grandma in the first act, and she hadn't died until the second. It was then that I felt that I had a future with the drama groups. I had several good parts over the years in plays and pantomimes as this acting lark had become second nature.

Then came the big one. We were to do a one-off play, *A Midsummer Night's Dream* by that author of all authors, William Shakespeare. I was to play the part of Puck, one of the fairies. Ah well, I thought, how difficult can it be, I had done it in the ring for 14 years so I must be halfway there before we start. Anyway, God knows what the script meant, I couldn't help but notice that it was all Thees and Thous, and what the hell was a dewlap? and an Ass's Knoll? It must have been written in a Brummie accent I thought. I knew Billy Shakespeare was thought to have been born in Stratford but maybe he was an overspill playwright from Dudley. Well, that was my opinion anyway.

It was decided that we should all take a day out and go and see this play, done properly by the Royal Shakespeare Company, on their home turf in Stratford. I must say that to me, whose knowledge of Shakespeare was somewhat limited and my interest somewhat less, I have to say that it was fantastic. I laughed so much that I had to take a couple of days off work due to strained stomach muscles. Then came the rehearsals, which turned out to be rather more interesting than I had thought possible. We were to do this play on a midsummer night out in the open and in the gardens of a rather grand house. The powers that be had decided that Puck would make one of his entrances leading a real donkey on stage and that we would use a smoke machine to give the right atmosphere for the famous sword fight. It worked fine during every rehearsal as the smoke would always flow to the warmest part, this being the large house at the back of the stage area, leaving a misty backdrop to the scene.

However, on the night of the show, fate was against us. The donkey dropped his load in the centre of the stage, only for me to step barefoot into it during the next scene. The smoke had now decided that the warmest place to drift was over the whole audience. We couldn't see them, and they couldn't see us. We had to stop the show for ten minutes until it cleared, much to the amusement of the audience. What was that old saying? Never work with children and animals.

My next major role was in the musical *Andy Capp,* written by Trevor Peacock, best known for playing Jim 'No no no yes' Trott in the Vicar of Dibley, with music by Alan Price, a famous musician of the day. I was Andy Capp, a part that I particularly enjoyed, and I was partnered with Rebecca Anning, a great actress, who played the part of Flo.

We had a great musical director and stage director; the whole cast was quality. What could possibly go wrong?

Well, I must put my hand up to a couple of little mistakes (it wouldn't have made this book otherwise, would it?) My first was my opening line to a barmaid. My line was 'Hello darling, where did you get that cute little nose and those big brown eyes?' 'They came with my head' was her reply. My first line of the first show. What I actually said was, 'Hello darling, where did you get those cute little eyes and that big brown nose?'

My second blip came in the third act when a pub fight broke out and I was supposed to turn around and punch the rent man. This I did as rehearsed, not touching him. I distinctly felt the whiskers on his chin. Too close for comfort, another eighth of an inch and I would have decked him. Dear old Ian, he never let me forget it. Overall, it went well for seven performances with no other snags. At least none that I know of.

It was many years later when I bid farewell to Priors Players and joined another group who called themselves the Burdock Valley Players. I had met several of their members previously at the local drama festival, and I knew they were good as they always seemed to win most of the trophies and in several categories. They were serious contenders for drama in general and took it rather more seriously than yours truly. I would give it my best attempt, but would they take me seriously?

It didn't help when one of them asked me what drama I had done previously, and I replied that I had been a leading light in the Great Otley and Netterton Amateur Dramatics Society. 'Wow' they replied. Then I had to spoil it by saying, 'Oh yes, I was always known for being very big in the G.O.N.A.D.S.'

All in all, I enjoyed my time with them and made some great friends along the way, once they had got used to my sense of humour. We were doing a Christmas production of *Scrooge,* and yes, I was he. Sixty-one pages of dialogue and twelve songs to learn and if that wasn't bad enough there were only four tunes for all the songs.

Rehearsals were great fun though and I said to one young lady cast member that I didn't think her costume was right as in that period that it was set in, I was sure that they didn't wear bustles around their bums. 'Cheeky sod, I'm not wearing a bustle,' she replied.

It didn't seem to upset her though as a couple of years later, she became my wife, and the best friend I have ever had. In the play, she owed me ten shillings, which as I keep reminding her, I never got. The show went well apart from the fact that on the opening night I developed a minor chest infection which then gave me my excuse for my poor singing. It turned out to be a successful run and I don't remember many gremlins except for John Slingsby, who was playing Jacob Marley. He entered the stage all bandaged with great big heavy chains binding him from head to foot and managed to get some of his chains stuck in the staging. He delivered his lines perfectly whilst tugging away at those damn chains and finally managed to get free, but he managed to pull up a part of the stage, which went back down with one hell of a bang.

All this, and I was expected to keep a straight face. I must say that I was fortunate in being able to play several roles over the years, But I have to say that the one that I enjoyed the most was playing Rene in the stage version of *Allo Allo*.

It all happened when I happened to mention to the Director, Phil Ray, that if he was stuck for casting the show, then I would be willing to take some small part if it would help him out. Next thing I hear is that I was cast in the biggest part in the whole show. I must admit that I went into a panic when I read the script. There was a hell of a lot to learn, and I was getting older, so the brain was not as good at remembering lines.

The rehearsals would start in a months' time. My mind went into overload so much that by the first rehearsal, I knew my lines for the first and second acts and what's more I started rehearsals in full costume which, as far as I know, was unheard of in the world of am dram. I stayed with drama for many years after that, wrote ten pantomimes, directed several plays and wrote two musicals, *A Nightingale Sang* and *Sherlock Holmes, the musical*.

The Boys

Apart from the drama, there is nothing I appreciate more than spending an evening in the presence of the Treorchy Male Voice Choir. I mentioned them in my first book and saw them for the first time when I was a mere seventeen years of age. I have travelled all over to see them and seen them perform in their own town of Treorchy and in their own Theatre three times so far, it doesn't get any better than that.

Whenever I do that trip, I take a short diversion and visit the little village of Aberfan to pay my respects. Some older ones among us will never forget that awful disaster when a coal slag heap collapsed and covered a primary school, killing many children and some teachers, a memory that will always be seared into my memory. Then it's on to that mecca of song, Treorchy and the Parc and Dare theatre to hear the best male choir in the world ply their trade.

I take great pleasure in saying that I have become good friends with many of them over the years. I remember seeing them in Gloucester Cathedral, they were fantastic as usual. During the interval, I joined a few of them outside. It was then that I was invited to join them after the show a few miles away for a drink or two (maybe more) by one of my choir friends, John Fletcher. We got chatting and my time as a wrestler came up. I happened to mention to John that I had written a book about my wrestling career titled 'Confessions of a Wrestler' and that I would send him a copy the following day.

We carried on chatting and then a couple of the choir decided to start singing, followed by a few more, and then the whole choir started to give an impromptu performance. Believe me when I tell you that no amount of money could ever have bought that feeling I had, listening to them sing again in the privacy of that cricket club bar room, late at night, in the wilds of somewhere in Gloucestershire.

Since then, I have become friends with others, among them Alan Bowen, Mark Milsom, Mark Williams, David Bebb and many more. At one of their after-show drink-in's, In the village of Whitchurch in Hampshire, the choir awarded me with a lot of their merchandise and thanked me for my support over the years and for the piece that I had written about them in my first book. Again the drink was flowing, and the singing soon began again.

Another wonderful evening in the company of great guys, friends and yes, legends in my opinion. I last saw them in a church in Tidworth which coincided with seeing them live fifty times. They kindly presented me with a framed photo of all the boys which hangs proudly in my house.

I think I must be the oldest groupie ever. In all that time, listening to and becoming good friends with many of the choir has become a most important fixture in my life, and, of course, there is nothing more enjoyable than having a few beers with 'the boys' after a successful concert. I can't wait until the next time.

Spending time with some of 'The Boys' of the Treorchy Male Choir, during the interval of another fantastic concert.

A Not So Brief Encounter

As a wrestler, the time comes when you must hang up your boots, and there are many reasons for this – age, physical ability and family commitments to name but a few. My reason was the latter, combined with the fact that wrestling was soon going to be taken off the television and to me, I felt that was the death knoll of wrestling. It took a further few years but eventually, it was gone. Certainly it was the end of the Golden Era as we all knew it. It wasn't long before I had lost touch with nearly all my wrestling buddies and with the death of my good friend Pat Roach, I think I had finally put my wrestling years firmly behind me. Of course, there were many times when ny memories would come back to me, and I would spend time reminiscing about the good old days. Usually, it was when someone asked me if I had known some wrestler that they had seen or met in their wanderings. It was during those moments that I came to realize how much I missed those days and what great friends I had made at the time. Of course, I could always stage a comeback, that is if the promoters were willing to fit a stairlift to the ring. No – those days for me were well and truly gone forever.

Looking on the bright side, I had managed to carve out a new career and one that would see me through to my retirement and beyond if the good Lord allows, so I considered myself one of the lucky ones. I stopped wrestling in 1983, and about 30 years later a chance meeting brought the world of wrestling back into my life.

I had read in the newspapers of the passing of that father of wrestling Mick McManus. Like many people in the business, I had a lot of respect for him. As a household name and a good wrestler, I felt I would attend his funeral, so I took myself off to Woking, in Surrey.

I wondered if by any chance I might meet up with someone I would have known back in the day. If so, would I recognize them and would they recognize me? Only time would tell. I had never felt so stunned in my life. There must have been well over forty wrestlers there. Some I recognized straight away but the majority I was struggling to put names to.

Then Tony 'Banger' Walsh came up and said, 'I might be wrong but aren't you the Glitterboy?' 'Oh yes' I said, as I shook hands. He continued, 'I haven't seen you since we worked for Evan Trehearne, must have been 30 years ago.'

He turned away. 'Hey Frank, come and see who I've got here.' And so, it went on. By the end of the funeral, I reckon that I had shaken hands and chatted to everyone there. I must now confess, and I don't want to sound disrespectful, that I don't know when I enjoyed myself at a funeral so much as I did that day.

Before I left for my homeward journey, someone said, 'Why don't we see you at any of the reunions?' 'What reunions.'? I replied blankly. 'I don't know anything about any reunions.' 'Give me your telephone number and I'll let you know the date of the next one.' 'That would be great, and I'll try to make it.' And that was how I became an avid supporter of the reunion movement.

Four months later, on a Sunday morning, I was on my way to a small village in Kent to attend my first reunion. It was held at the village pub in a pretty location called South Darenth. The owners of the venue were none other than the past heavyweight world champion Wayne Bridges and his lovely wife Sarah. Sarah was a world renowned bodybuilder in her time. The pub was called the Bridges, but to this day, I'm not sure if it had been named after them or perhaps it might be something to do with the fact that it had been built in the shadow of a massive viaduct carrying trains to London. Either way, it was a lovely part of the world to visit and if I managed to renew old acquaintances, then it promised to be a great day.

As usual, I arrived about two hours early as I had no idea about the traffic on the M25. The first person I met was Barry, a wrestler I had never met before, but we soon found out that we both knew a lot of the same people from our past, so the time went rather quickly.

Later on many wrestlers and their families began to arrive and true to tradition, I was roped in to erecting a gazebo. What a fiasco that was. There were a dozen of us trying to get this damn thing up. Honestly, I thought, I knew the time when with half the number of wrestlers, we could have put up a wrestling ring in twenty minutes and here we were, sweating, swearing and generally moaning trying to erect this gazebo. It eventually took us about an hour and a half. To be fair, we discovered that two gazebos of different sizes had been stored together, so at least we felt vindicated from too much embarrassment.

Then came the most wonderful news of all. The tea van was open. I had been dying for a cuppa all morning. As I sat there, tea and a bacon roll in hand and chatting to Karl Heinz, a wrestler of the first order, and catching up on old times, we were joined by Johnny Kincaid, who, as many people know, was one of my all-time heroes, and then along came Tony Scarlo, who I had known many years previously in my early career when we, along with his brother Joey, worked for the promoter Orig Williams. From that moment on, I must confess that this whole situation had taken me back and, in my mind, I was 17 years old again. The old banter was just as good as it had been all those years ago. We must have been chatting and reminiscing for quite a while and it struck me why the world of wrestling was always known as the grunt and groan game when we all tried to get up from our seats. The first one up was the winner, and his reward was to help the rest of us up onto our feet.

It was time to mingle and relive a few more of those precious memories before the time came for that well respected wrestler Colin Joynson to read out the obituaries, and to do what is affectionately known as the ten-bell count followed by two minutes' silence. Following this came the awards, given out for wrestlers and for those who had made their mark in the world of wrestling. Every one of those awards was well deserved in my opinion and showed the level of respect given by many of those who had played their own part in making the golden years of wrestling special. The reminiscing and the beer flowed all afternoon.

No drink for me as I was driving, but the tea kept coming and made for the best afternoon I had spent in a long time. I also managed to get a few words with Frank Rimer who had been rushing around making sure that the reunion went without a hitch as this whole day had been organized by him, along with Wayne and Sarah Bridges.

Frank had been a wrestler but had made his name as a Master of Ceremonies in his later years. He also, along with Tony Scarlo, started a well-used and respected wrestling training gym called Dropkix, which turned out some fine wrestlers during its day.

My final throw of the dice was bumping into Hack, who, along with his mate Anglo, were the owners/organisers of the world-renowned wrestling fan website Wrestling Heritage. A few months earlier they had kindly added me to the A to Z list of wrestlers. Little did I know that our paths would cross many times in the future. Hack, whose real name is Alan, has done more to keep the golden years of wrestling alive than anyone I know.

As I said my farewells and wended my way home, I thought back to how many wrestling buddies I had met up with throughout the day. Big names in the business along with some lesser-known wrestlers, every one of them the salt of the earth. There was Johnny Kincaid, Mal Sanders, Karl Heinz, Jackie Pallo Jnr, Steve Veidor, Johnny Saint, Johnny Kidd, Brian Maxine and oh so many more. When I arrived home, I shared my day with my wife Ruth, and I must have gone on for about a week. Anecdote after anecdote, name after name that didn't mean a damn thing to my good lady as by the time we met, my wrestling career had been over for many years. She took it all in good part and never yawned once, bless her.

'One day I will take you and introduce you to all of them,' I enthused. Her eyeballs went up to the ceiling and I knew it was time to shut up. I had quite a few telephone numbers of these old friends and kept in touch with most. I knew I would be seeing them again at the next reunion or, heaven forbid, the next funeral.

None of us are getting any younger and we are at that stage of life when some of us may not make it to the next reunion and may be called to that great changing room in the sky. However, God willing, I shall be there next year and every year after that. I must state here that this first reunion was my inspiration to put pen to paper and write my first book, 'Confessions of a wrestler'. Could I do it, I thought to myself? Then I read two excellent books written by my good friend Johnny Kincaid and that did the trick.

I think it was a couple of reunions later when I was to receive my first award, which was the Services to Wrestling award. A proud moment, as it was presented to me by the legend of wrestling, Mr Alan Sargeant, whose wrestling skills I had admired for many years in my youth when I would sit on the floor and watch the wrestling on the television with my family, long before I entered the square circle for the first time. This skilful mat man presenting me with an award. Could it get any better? I didn't think so at the time.

My first award for services to wrestling

I remember this reunion vividly because having looked at the small amount of wrestling memorabilia that was on show, Big Daddy's leotards and ring capes, jackets once owned by Ski-Hi-Lee and a few other bits and pieces mainly on loan for the day by other wrestlers and fans, I was dismayed at the way it was just thrown onto a table like a WI jumble sale. Something had to be done and yours truly decided that these items of historic interest needed to be displayed properly and to be given the respect that they deserved. After many telephone discussions with Frank Rimer, the reunion organizer, I designed and built a mock-up wrestling ring using some old gazebo poles, bits of drainpipe and many rolls of coloured electrical tape, a sheet of white canvas and some corner pads. Now all I had to do was to build the display stands.

During this time, Mick McManus's son Tony had donated some of Mick's trophies, his ring leotards and wrestling boots with the proviso that they should be sold to help the reunion funds. They were sent to a specialist sports auction in Chippenham to be sold to the highest bidder. That was it, I thought. They are mine. When the day of the sale arrived, off I went to Wessex Auctions and had made up my mind that I wasn't coming home without them.

I arrived early, as I always seemed to, and waited a couple of hours in the car until they finally opened the doors. In I went and straight to the table where the items were displayed, a quick check over then off to get a cuppa.

Eventually, we all took our seats for the Auction. Here comes lot one. I looked in the catalogue and saw that Mick's lot was no. 350. My chin hit the floor. There was only one thing for it, back to the tearoom for another cuppa. Three cups later and a trip to the loo, I returned to the Auction just in time to see lot 36 go under the hammer. This is going to be a long day, I thought. Eventually, the lot

I was after came up. The internet bidders were ready as were the telephone bidders. That's it, I'm going to have to sell a kidney.

Eventually, I managed to come away with the goodies in the boot and the wallet into rehab, but I had done it. Now what? Yes, you've guessed it. I donated the stuff back to the reunion that had been forced to sell it in the first place. That's what I had intended all along. Now I would have to make a display case for it.

It was during this time that I received a phone call from Frank telling me that Wayne Bridges had donated four trophies that he had won during his time in the ring and when they were polished up, could I please make another four display cabinets. He sent me the measurements and I ordered more wood, Perspex and lining fabric. It took me several weeks of being in the workshop until late and towards the end I thought I had turned into Geppetto, Pinocchio's dad. In the meantime, Frank had been polishing away to get some life and recognition into the trophies. They had been left in a garage for many years and were barely recognizable. A frantic phone call from Frank, late one night revealed that the first one wasn't one of Wayne's but had belong to another wrestler called Prince Kumali. Over the next few weeks and another three phone calls later, it turned out that none of them belonged to Wayne but were all Kumali's. Ah well, at least he was a world-famous wrestler, so it would make no difference.

A few weeks later Frank had managed to get a pair of boots that belonged to Mike Marino and a few other bits and pieces, all of which needed displaying so that was it, more wood, Perspex and lining fabric. This in turn led to more time in the bloody workshop. My wife must have thought I had left home.

Eventually, after several attempts at assembling things with the help of my daughter Donna, who was coming to the next reunion to help her poor old dad setting everything up, we were all ready. Then the reunion was upon us. I managed to finally get it all into the car the night before with the aid of my long-suffering wife and thought I would go and get petrol. Bugger, the car wouldn't start. I tried frantically ringing around to see if I could borrow one, but no joy. You certainly know who your friends are in a situation like that.

My wife had an idea. 'You will have to take mine.'

'What, the bloody Mini? How the hell are we going to get it all in that?'

'We can but try' she replied.

The Angels must have been smiling on me that night because she was right. It was a tight fit but hey, who needs first gear anyway? It was fortunate that Frank was bringing the bulky cabinets. I had the lucky foresight to take the cabinets down to his house a few days before. Finally, we arrived at the venue, okay, two hours early but that's what I do, I guess. Anyway, we needed extra time so that we could set up and it's a good job we were early because I couldn't remember where it all went. However, we did manage it with time left over for a cup of tea and a bacon roll.

I think, overall, it was a success, and everyone seemed to enjoy and appreciate the effort. I had also produced a brochure detailing what was on display and who had loaned it for the day and so forth. It was great fun talking to people and answering all their questions. Mind you, a lot of the fans knew more about the wrestlers' careers than I did, as was often the case. Over the next year or so, it went from strength to strength as more items were presented or loaned to the reunion. We even had a mask donated to the reunion by that well known wrestler Kendo Nagasaki, who, of course presented it in a way that only kendo could by doing some sort of mystic ritual and setting fire to it and then putting it out again. The significance of that escapes me to this day. But we were glad of the mask, which would take pride of place in our little venture and yes, another bloody display case.

I took the mask home with me in order to display it to its best ability and ordered a black display polystyrene head which came the next day. What I am about to tell you might seem a bit far-fetched and fanciful, but I promise you, every word of it is true.

The mask had not been in our house for more than two days when my wife said that it gave her the creeps, so would I take it out of the dining room and put it out in the utility room. I laughed at her but when I could see that it had really affected her, I moved it out. During that week we had seven lightbulbs blow, the boiler went wrong, two remote controls went flat even though the batteries were only a week old, my alarm clock went off early one morning and it hadn't been set and to top it all, a pane of glass in the utility room exploded.

Now this may have been coincidence, but I wasn't taking any chances. I rang Ken, who was part of the reunion, and asked him if he could take it, explaining my predicament. He laughed at me but agreed to take it so without any delay, I put the display case in the car and did the seventy-mile round trip.

It was a while later when I next spoke to him and he told me that he and his wife had experienced much the same things as we had, so he had taken it to his dad's and put it in the garage out of the way. It was present at the next reunion and took its rightful place on the exhibition stand, but after that, it was kept along with the other items upstairs in the pub.

At the reunion the following year I was informed that all the exhibition items had been removed to a museum in Croydon. The Fairfield Halls, a popular venue for wrestling and one of the places used to film for the television bouts, was being closed and a new venue was built on another site. The powers that be had it in mind to turn the old place into a museum depicting all the past entertainment that had gone on in the building over the years displaying items of interest, and of course wrestling had played a major part there over the years. It never actually happened, and the idea was later shelved. Too late for us to revive it unfortunately, but it was time to move on.

The reunion lasted a couple more years during which, in a very short time Wayne Bridges sadly passed away and a while later Frank Rimer died and Sarah Bridges died later. It was inevitable that the Southern Wrestlers' Reunion would soon, after thirty years, cease to be. Ken Sowden, who had helped to run the reunion in the latter days did his best to keep it going, but it was a losing battle. Ken, however, went on to ply his organizing talent in another way within the world of wrestling. More of that later. It finally closed in 2021. Too soon in my opinion.

As with all the wrestlers that has passed away over the years, this reunion will be sadly missed. A dedicated group of people have resurrected it many miles away and only time will tell of its success. I cannot comment on it because I have, so far, never attended.

The Reunion Exhibits with Johnny Kidd and the author

FUNERAL OF A LEGEND

In 2015 the world lost that great wrestler Pete Szakacs, brother of the late Tibor Szakacs. Having met Pete many years ago and indeed learned a lot from him during a couple of pull rounds, I felt it was the right thing to go and pay my respects at his funeral. The service was taking place in Milton Keynes, a fair drive away, but I was determined to attend.

I arrived in good time and even found a little café across the road that served a lovely cup of tea. It wasn't long before I was joined outside the church by Johnny Kidd, a skilful wrestler who I had met a couple of years previous. I guess it was a sign of the times that although the church was packed, we were the only two wrestlers there. The service went on and on. I reckon it was nearly two hours' worth. I remember thinking to myself, if they don't hurry up, it will hardly be worth me going home.

When it had finished, it was a case of following the car in front to the nearby crematorium where another service would take place. As I entered the waiting area, I saw my old mate Johnny Kincaid sitting there. Mmm, I thought, he's not daft. He knew the church service would be a long affair so he had decided to wait at the crematorium.

A relatively short service took place, and we soon found ourselves outside and the three of us chatted for a while. Eventually, Johnny Kidd had to go as he had to get back to work, and then there was two of us. 'What shall we do now?' I asked. 'I don't know' he said. 'Well, I reckon we should find a pub.' 'Do you think we should?'

'I think it would be rude not to. This is your patch mate do you know of a decent place?'

'Follow me.' He jumped into his car and I into mine.

Johnny shot off at some speed and I tried my hardest to keep up. That journey was like Formula One with roundabouts as I tried to keep up. Roundabout after roundabout later, there were four cars between us. If I lose him now, I'm buggered, I thought. Then it dawned on me that perhaps it would have been a good idea to ask him the name of the pub.

Eventually, the number of cars between us had dropped to two just as he pulled into a pub car park. I followed him and managed to find a spot to park. When we got out, he said to me 'Do you recognise this place?'

I said 'I'm not sure. Should I?'

'It's the pub that's on the front cover of my last book. It's called the Bletchley Arms now but when I had the pub it was called Kincaid's.'

'Bloody hell, that's a coincidence,' I said.

'You daft pillock' came the reply, 'It was named that after I moved in.' Then it dawned on him that I was joking, and he smiled and shook his head. We spent an hour or so before I had to leave to get home. It was a pleasure spending time in such good company, and it wouldn't be the last time, as you will read later in the book.

A Kiss Me Quick Hat and a Stick of Rock

In 2016 I learned that another reunion was to start in Blackpool and of course, I was very interested. This would not just mean a day out but living in the south, a whole weekend away, which would mean two whole days of wrestle talk and reminiscing. Coupled with the fact that I would meet up with more wrestlers from the north-east who I hadn't seen for years, I couldn't wait. This reunion was put together by Jackie McCann and her good friend Val Hardy. Jackie had been on the wrestling scene for many years and was, without doubt, one of the finest female wrestlers there has ever been.

In early May I found myself on a long train journey to that famous seaside place Blackpool. As I have got older, I am less inclined to drive long journeys, which is strange for someone who has spent many years driving all over the UK. Now if it's over three hours' drive, that's me on the train. And as far as luxury goes, I always travel first class. If I can't do it at my time of life, then when can I?

Nowadays, as I have hit three score and ten and my legs have all but given up, I take advantage of Passenger Assistance, which means that I no longer manage to walk from one platform to another, so they send a buggy or a wheelchair to collect me at every station. It is a reliable and helpful system and what's more, it's all free.

After a five-hour journey with only three changes, I finally arrived at my destination. A quick taxi ride and I was at my guest house. I looked up and down the street and tried to remember how it was the last time I was here. It must be forty-two years ago, but nothing had changed, at least on the outside. I hoped it had changed on the inside. I remembered the old Blackpool landladies of the day, and formidable didn't cover it. They ruled with a rod of iron. If you made a noise when you came in late, you would hear about it in the morning, but if she had to come down and let you in after she had retired for the night, look out. If you had downed a few beers and plucked up the courage to answer her back, you might as well slash your wrists there and then. I only did it once.

'I don't like opening the door in my dressing gown' she says.

'I didn't know you had a door in your dressing gown,' I replied. Big mistake. My breakfast was thrown on the table the next morning as she walked away mumbling to herself 'bloody theatricals' (that's what us wrestlers were often called.) As I went in, I couldn't have been more mistaken – warm, friendly and welcoming. and the room had its own bathroom with a shower. Great, no padding along the corridors in the night to the loo.

I got settled in and went down to the bar area, where I met Jackie and Val for the first time. 'Hello' said a voice from behind me. 'My name's Gerry, I've never wrestled but I am a great fan.' 'Pleased to meet you Gerry, I'm Martin, the Glitterboy'.

He turned out to be a nice bloke did Gerry, as gay as they come and a built-in comedian as well.

That's it I thought, as he took a fancy to me, that is until a few minutes later when Les Prest and the other lads from the north-east arrived. Then I lost Gerry's affections to Les, who seemed to be a better bet than me. From that moment on Gerry always referred to me as Glitterballs. I didn't mind, it didn't matter what he said to you, you could never take offence. It was great to meet up with Les, Jimmy 'Boy' Devlin, Dickie Swales, Sean McNeil and the one and only Sam Betts. I had fought a few times in the north-east all those years ago so I had met a few of them before. I remember fighting with Jimmy Boy Devlin a couple of times. He was a great worker but would on occasions get over excited. One night, he threw me so hard out of the ring that I thought I was going to have to pay to get back in the hall. Since that first meet up again with Jimmy, I have had the pleasure of meeting him now on several occasions. We speak regularly on the phone and when we are together at reunions. He sidles up to me and says quietly, 'Tell them about when I threw you out the ring.' We spend a lot of time ribbing and generally goading each other. All in good fun though. In my book, the sign of a good friendship.

Sadly, a few months after this reunion we got the sad news that Gerry had passed away; he is sadly missed by all who knew him. All in all, it was a great weekend and a great reunion. I was glad that I had decided to make that trip to Blackpool and looked forward to the next time. Several years have passed since that first reunion, and I still attend and look forward to it every year.

Back row Lt to Rt. The Glitterboy, Les Prest, Jimmy 'Boy' Devlin. Front row: Sam Betts, Dickie Swales, Sean McNeil.

Dickie Swales, sadly no longer with us, was the joker of the pack. He would come out with one-liners like they were going out of fashion. I asked him once 'whereabouts do you live Dickie?' His reply, 'Next to the canal, you must drop in some time.' I called Sam Betts the one and only on the previous page and that is exactly what he is. He had a wrestling career spanning many decades, seen it all and done it all, but I have never met such a modest person in my life, and a pure gentleman. He has earned, deserves and gets respect from not only myself but from more wrestlers than anyone I have ever met. Sir. I salute you.

Sean is a quiet and retiring sort of guy who tends to stay in the background. Nevertheless he could take his rightful place beside any wrestler and has done more that his fair share of travelling up and down the country to add to the pleasure of the avid wrestling fans.

The next day was the day of the reunion at the Royal British Legion. The hall was decked, the buffet was prepared, and people were arriving. To my delight I had met up with Hack from the Heritage web site, so we had a good natter, as you do. This followed by meeting up after many years with another ring legend, Alan Kilbey, and his lovely daughter Tracey. Those who remember Alan will know that he and Tracey are deaf, but I had two cousins who were both deaf, so our communications were not a problem. It was good to see that Alan had not lost his sense of humour and we spent a while laughing with some of the memories that we shared.

Tracey asked me if I had ever wrestled with her dad. I shook my head and through sign language told her I had been on the same bill. On the posters he was top of the bill with his name made up of three-inch letters and my name was at the bottom next to the ticket prices with letters of about half an inch high. She thought it was hilarious. It was always a pleasure to be in their company, two lovely people.

I also had the pleasure of meeting up with a first-rate lady wrestler, Naughty Nancy Barton, or to use her real name, Ann Barton. She used to live not far from me when I was a teenager, and I surprised her when I told her that I remembered her from my younger days when she served me my first pint in a local pub.

With the turnout, I knew that this reunion would go from strength to strength. Those who were staying for another night took off for the traditional Chinese meal which, as I remember, was always a ritual in the old days. It had been a good weekend, and I also picked up a second services to wrestling award. Another memorable moment and yes, I would be back next year. I had met many wrestlers from my past and a lot of fans at this first of what would turn out to be many Blackpool reunions.

Another award for my services to wrestling

The author with Lt. Jackie McCann and Naughty Nancy Barton

As I write this today, the Blackpool reunion has, as expected, has grown considerably over the years and is now one of the biggest in the UK. It has had to move from venue to venue in order to cater for the number of visitors. It has also been necessary to move accommodation for the same reason.

We now hold it in a large hotel where there are more rooms, and it can also cater for the reunion, which makes life that much easier for the organisers. I have also had the privilege of serving on the committee for a time as treasurer which I was proud to do. However, due to a few health problems, I had to stand down.

The reunion is in safe hands with a good solid committee behind it and stands in a good position to run and run.

North of the Border Take 2

It was during one of the Blackpool reunions that I met up with some wrestlers from Ayrshire in Scotland. We got on well and as I had wrestled there many times over the years and once visited the local training gym, I had decided to attend one of their reunions. Several of us made the journey north.

A while later I received a telephone call from Johnny Kincaid asking how I was travelling up to Ayr. 'I've got an idea' he said, 'Why don't you drive up to my place and we can go up together, stay at my daughter's overnight then on to the reunion, stay overnight in the hotel then drive back to my daughter's for another night, then home the next day.'

'That sounds great mate, I'm up for that. I'll book a twin room at the hotel' I said, as I knew that we needed to book early as they get very busy, and I didn't want to leave it too late.

When the day arrived I had decided to take the train to Johnny's house as I remembered the last time I drove in Milton Keynes and to be honest, I lost my bottle. Of course, I had to travel to London, change stations and get another train, which took me longer than driving there, but it was my best option.

I took a short taxi ride to his house and as per usual, arrived a bit early. Enough time for a cup of tea which was nice, and I met Hazel, his wife, a lovely lady. Soon we were off on the first leg of our long journey. I have to say that Johnny is the best company on any journey. He is a born storyteller, sharing some of his stories of his past wrestling career and his time of wrestling abroad. I can honestly say that we laughed all the way there.

We finally arrived at his daughter's house. A lovely house indeed. You just felt the warmth and love in the house as soon as you entered. For an old wrestler who has laid his head in some suspect digs throughout his career, this was sheer luxury.

Unfortunately, Chera, Johnny's daughter, was not there as she was away with work, but her wife, Sarah, made us welcome with copious amounts of tea, a superb meal and a most comfortable bed. What more can a man want?

After a lovely breakfast in the morning we said our goodbyes and started on the final leg of our outbound journey. Apart from the banter and laughter between us the journey was uneventful – until we were about five miles from Ayr. Then we got lost. I have no idea where we went wrong but it took us about ninety minutes and around thirty-five miles to get to our hotel.

That's it, I thought, we are here, what else could go wrong? What else indeed. We booked in and eventually found our room. On entering we soon realised something. There was a double bed. I laughed my head off, but Johnny was having none of it and went off on one. 'I'm not having it, it's not happening!' he shouted at the top of his voice as he stormed off to the reception.

That was it, I couldn't resist it, I immediately went into my old wrestling persona. 'Oh Johnny, don't go on so, you'll upset me.'

He said nothing and marched into the reception area with me mincing behind him, much to the amusement of some of the wrestlers who had already cottoned on to what was happening. Within minutes, the hotel staff had gone to the room and split the beds (as I knew they would). Then Johnny came down from the ceiling and started to see the funny side of the situation. He was ribbed by everyone there over the weekend but took it all in good humour. We wrestlers chatted amongst ourselves until it was time to head out for an evening meal that had kindly been laid on by the reunion committee at a place of their choice somewhere in town. We were picked up by a wrestler known as Ian 'Teddy Bear' Taylor, who had kindly volunteered his services and his car for the duration. Ian was a local lad who was a good wrestler back in the day, and he would become a good friend to me, as you will hear later. The meal was excellent and our friends from the Wrestlers' Reunion Scotland did us proud and looked after us as only the Scottish people can.

I remember only too well that when I worked there all of those years ago, at least one local wrestler on the bill would come up and say, 'Have you got a place to stay tonight? If not, you can stay at mine. Big breakfast in the morning and then you can get on your way when you're ready.' If you took him up on his generous offer, he would quickly ring his wife or mum, and they would make you up a bed for the night. It didn't matter where in Scotland you were wrestling, that always seemed to happen. It was gratifying that after all those years, they were still as accommodating as they ever were. Even now, I always look forward to my annual trip up to that great land and the friends that I have there.

It was a very enjoyable reunion, and I was proud and yet pleasantly surprised to receive yet another award. This time, it was a Legend of the Ring award and the icing on the cake was that it was presented to me by none other than my mate Mr Johnny Kincaid. I have never made any secret of the fact that when I was about twelve years old, he was a hero of mine, and to be honest, he still is. And he had presented me with this award – wow, stick a fork in me, I'm done. How often does a hero go on later in life to become a friend? Yes, this reunion was a great success and, God willing, I will be coming back.

We said our goodbyes to everyone as the day ended and we had to get back to that warm comfortable bed at Johnny's daughter's, where we spent the night before heading home again. As we approached the outskirts of Milton Keynes Johnny asked me what time my train was. I didn't know, but could he drop me at the station, I would get the next train to London then change stations to my next change, Clapham Junction.

'I'll do better than that, I'll take you straight to Clapham.'

'But you are nearly home' I said.

'That's okay, no problem.'

So off we set for London. It was a very interesting journey as Johnny went the long way round and showed me some of the places where he had grown up and worked, which to me was interesting. The next time I read his books I could now put a visible face to the things he had written about.

Eventually we arrived at Clapham Station and after I had insisted on giving him some petrol money, we said our farewells. Luckily, I had only a ten-minute wait for a train that would take me directly to my own village station.

It had been a fantastic weekend and one I shall always remember. We have since been back to the Ayr reunion several times now and a couple of years ago, they gave me the great honour of asking me if I would become Honorary President of the Wrestlers' Reunion Scotland. A great honour indeed.

I was talking to Johnny last week as we are sharing a room again in September, single beds of course. Unfortunately, I am unable to travel up with him as now I am getting older and I am prone to getting the odd deep vein thrombosis, so the doctor has warned me about long journeys by car. At least I'll be able to get up and walk about on the train. Shame really, but we must make sacrifices as we get older and less mobile.

I was honoured to have been asked to become Honorary President, an offer that I readily accepted. Even today I feel honoured to have been given this most prestigious post.

These are the three reunions I have regularly attended. I would be failing in my duty if I didn't mention that there are others available – Leeds, Manchester and others I don't know about. All tend to be one-day affairs and too far for me to travel to but nevertheless, too important not to mention.

I would like to tell you now of some more memorable and humorous moments that have happened to me over the years.

I Need a Snorkel

One night at the Blackpool reunion, a group of about four of us decided to go out for a meal. We ordered a taxi, and all piled in, Rex Lane in the front, real name Barry, and I was in the back next to his wife Lisa. Now there was a bit of a squeeze in the back and believe me when I tell you that it was by pure accident, that I ended up with my face firmly jammed in Lisa's ample bosom. If I tell you that it was most uncomfortable, you won't believe me, so I won't. Someone said, and I couldn't see who, 'Are you okay Glitterboy?' I mumbled something, but even I couldn't understand what I had replied. I just heard the laughter from my so-called friends. Barry said in a flat voice, 'If we go over any bumps he'll have two black eyes in the morning.' Even the taxi driver was laughing.

Finally, we reached our destination, and everyone piled out. I had to wait for Barry to come round and open the door before I could back out the taxi and disengage my face from his wife's boobs. 'Thank god. I can breathe again. By the way Lisa when you go to bed tonight, if you find a pair of glasses and my hearing aid, let me have them back in the morning. That moment was never forgotten by any of us and is mentioned often.

Have You Got a Light Boy?

It was in Blackpool that Val had brought along her daughter and granddaughters to the reunion. The oldest of her granddaughters had some stick-on eyelashes with a view to putting them on Val, but she wasn't having any of it.

'Okay, put them on me,' I said. I didn't mind looking a fool in a good cause, after all, I had been looking like a fool with make-up on for years in the past. She put them on me and did a couple more wrestlers as well. Hardly anyone noticed it so eventually, I had forgotten all about it, until a few hours later I went outside for a cigarette. I smoked roll-ups in those days, and I rolled the tobacco whilst chatting to someone, I can't remember who. I lit up and then it hit me, it tasted horrible, like burning glue. I had been smoking a rolled-up eye lash which had obviously fallen off into my tobacco. They say that smoking is bad for you, that one wasn't good. It could only happen to me.

Another time in Scotland, several of us again were piling into a car that my mate Ian was driving, heading for the centre of Ayr, for a meal out with all the other wrestlers. The car was looking quite full when it was my turn to get in. I am not as agile as I once was, so it took me some time. I was seated but still had one leg out when Ian decided to drive off.

The door was still half open and my leg was still out when I noticed that just ahead, there was a signpost looming up. If this door hits that signpost then my leg's a goner. Luckily, with everyone shouting at Ian, including me, he stopped just in time. They all saw the funny side of it and so did I... eventually. I still rib Ian about that night and I think it's going to be a while before I forget it.

Menace On The Road

Back in Blackpool, it was decided that a few of us would take a walk down to the sea front and have a look around, maybe stop for a bit of lunch. We started off and by the time we had reached the front, my legs were playing up and were giving me a lot of pain. 'Hey chaps, I'm going to sit on the wall here and wait for you to come back, I can't walk any further.' so off they went, and I can say that I had never enjoyed a sit down so much before.

They came back in about 45 minutes, and I was well rested by then, so I managed to get to the café over the road and enjoyed a good lunch. When we came out, they all decided to take a walk up the other side to see what was there. I opted to get a taxi back to the hotel. The taxi driver thought it was a bit odd considering it was only a half-mile journey, but he was okay once I explained the situation.

I vowed then that it wasn't going to happen again and the following year, I hired a mobility scooter for the whole weekend. I was free to go where and when I liked. It was a great feeling. Now I would have to wait for them instead of them waiting for me.

Two good friends of mine, a mother and daughter, Wendy and Erika, were taking a walk down to the pier to listen to the man playing the organ whilst they were having a drink and asked me if I would like to meet them down there. Of course, I jumped at the chance as I am fond of live music and these two were always wonderful company. I set off about thirty minutes later with my scooter, feeling like I was as free as a bird.

We listened to the organist, had a lovely chat and my cup of tea was delightful. The time came when I had to leave and make my way back. There was only one snag, I had forgotten the way home. I took one wrong turning and was completely lost. I drove around for about an hour and to my horror, I found myself going over a flyover, unfortunately, there was no pathway. I looked behind me and to my dismay, I seemed to be holding up rather a lot of traffic. I felt as if I was in a sketch as Victor Meldrew as I said to myself, 'I don't bloody well believe it!'

After stopping several times, going into several shops to ask the way, I finally reached the hotel. It took me seven minutes to get to the pier and nearly two hours to get back. That will teach me to be overconfident. I don't know if you have ever been on a mobility scooter, but I felt every bump in the road and believe me, I had been over every bump in Blackpool, or it felt that way.

I must say that my legs were fine. I wish I could have said the same about my arse.

Calendar Boys

At the Blackpool reunion a couple of years ago, it was decided that the world of wrestling needed a calendar of old school wrestlers. If it was good enough for the Women's Institute, it was good enough for us. I had decided that I would wear a cheeky little ensemble consisting of a pair of sequined covered pair of trunks and a pink feather boa (what else would the Glitterboy wear?) I can tell you that

I looked a right prat, but who cares, I wouldn't be the only one. A couple of photographers were hired, and provisions were made for the shoot to be done the day before the next reunion. If I remember correctly, I was 'Mr June'.

The day of the shoot soon came around and we were assembled in the pool room of the hotel. I can still see Johnny Kincaid slithering around seductively on the pool table dressed in my pink feather boa. Don't worry JK, I won't put up the photos. Finally, we were introduced to the photographers, a young chap and his girlfriend, and the shoot was going to take place in one of the rooms upstairs in the hotel.

We were taken into the makeshift studio, and I was first up. The look on the faces of the photographers was a picture as they had absolutely no idea what they were going to take photos of. They soon got the hang of it once their embarrassment had subsided and after about an hour, it was a wrap, as they say.

I may add that it had been many years since I'd seen my workmates in some of those positions and as it turns out, one of those memories that you can never erase from your mind.

It was several weeks later when the photographs arrived and I'm no prude but even I could see that they needed a fair bit of air brushing before they would be ready for publication. I got my daughter to do this task as my computer skills are not up to that sort of thing. She looked at the photos.

' Mmm, I don't think it will need to be much air brushing, are you sure you want to do a wrestler's calendar? you could just leave it as it is and do a Jurassic Park one.'

'You cheeky bugger' I replied.

However, she did a great job, and it was time to get it to the printers as time was running on and we needed to get them launched and sold well before the Christmas deadline. It all turned out okay and sales were brisk. We made enough to cover our expenses with a fair bit left over which, of course, went to the reunion's charity.

Would we do another? probably not, we are all a bit older and with the amount of clothes us oldies need to wear to keep warm now, it would take too long to do the shoot. Believe me (and I speak only for myself) when I go to bed at night, getting undressed is like playing pass the parcel.

A Grand Day Out in Watford

When the reunion in Kent closed its doors, it was decided by two wrestling friends that perhaps it would be a good idea to get the wrestlers together for a meal and another chance to reminisce about the old days, also, for us oldies to meet with today's wrestlers for a grand wrestlechattathon. (Yes, I know it's not a word, but it is now.)

The two responsible for putting together this event were Janjay Bagga, one of the top promoters of today's shows that you can see up and down the country, and Ken Sowden, of the old Kent reunion management. They decided that it would be by invitation only. (More of these two later.) It didn't take long before they realised that it was going to be so well received by all that the venue would not be big enough, so a bigger one was found. The venue was in Watford so it was central to all, as people would be attending from all over the UK.

One Sunday morning I was on my way up to Watford for the first of these events. Now I'm not familiar with this part of the country and

I thank the Lord for my satnav. I eventually arrived, having only been lost a few times, and was greeted by a voice that I was familiar with. 'If I'd known that you were invited, I wouldn't have come' shouted out Brian, better known in the wrestling world as Billy La Rue, closely followed by his wife Cathrine giving me a big hug.

I had first met up with this lovely couple in Scotland. I hadn't seen him for forty years when he tapped me on the shoulder in the hotel bar. 'You don't remember me do you?' he said 'No, I'm struggling,' I replied. 'I'm Billy La Rue' he said. I shook his hand 'If you had grabbed me by the arm and thrown me into that corner, I would have known you anywhere,' I said.

Later that year, they visited me at my home as they were passing on a visit to their daughter and it was, as always, a pleasure to see them. The whole event was well attended and believe me, well appreciated by everyone there.

I met and talked to people from the world of wrestling that I hadn't seen since I hung up my boots all those years ago. It was a great day, the meal was excellent, the company first class and I came away with memories that had completely skipped my mind. I can't wait until the next time.

What a Gay Day

Even though I hung up my boots around forty years ago, I still get asked about my wrestling days, and one question comes up more often than the others: why did you choose to wrestle as a gay boy? Before I start to answer this, I would just like to say that I never get annoyed at any questions about my days in the ring. After all, these questions come from the people or at least the people's children or even grandchildren of those that came to see me and others like me and helped to pay my wages. Without these diehard fans, I wouldn't have been able to do what I loved to do all those years ago and yes, I think we wrestlers owe them our gratitude.

The question is a fair one and I think needs to be answered truthfully. Before I chose my persona, I had done quite a bit of wrestling and to be fair, it was clear that I was never likely to be among the best wrestlers of the day. I was never going to be able to dazzle the crowd with my skill, so I decided that the only way I would make it in the business was to be a heel. It follows that I would have to have a gimmick or persona that would encourage the crowd to jeer at me, to laugh at me, to see me as a figure of fun to be ridiculed perhaps. I had seen the reaction many times on the television that people like John Inman, Larry Grayson and to some extent Danny La Rue had with their audiences. They made people laugh all the time with their body language and catchphrases like 'I'm free' and 'Shut that door.' The more the audience laughed, the more the audience seemed to take them to their heart, until most people loved to be entertained by them.

I'll have a piece of that, I thought to myself, so I sat one night with pen and paper and made a list of positives and negatives that came with such a persona. It wasn't a very long list, and I ended up screwing it up and throwing it in the bin. No, that wasn't going to work, so I decided to just dive in at the deep end and go for broke.

I gave myself a month before I felt I would be ready to face the public with my new image and have them accept me, but more importantly, for them to believe my persona.

I took a little bit of negativity from other wrestlers who thought that I had lost the plot, but once that they could see that the audiences were fascinated by that spectacle with long blonde hair, full make-up, flowing gowns and Lurex tights with silver sparkly boots, they seemed to accept it. Very soon, the audiences would laugh as I minced my way into the ring whilst blowing kisses to the young men in the room and poking my tongue out at their girlfriends. By the time I had entered the ring, they were jeering and by the second round with my, shall we say, unusual ring antics, most of them hated me.

What was even more of a result, more promoters were keen to put me on their books as by now, I was able to put bums on seats, which is the sort of language that was spoken by promoters as it meant more money for them. Let's not get carried away here, I wasn't some sort of star attraction, just a bloke whose wrestling ability, shall we say, wasn't up to a great standard and left a lot to be desired.

It was a bold decision, taken at a time when I felt unsure of my abilities, but I can honestly say that I never had occasion to regret it. There were of course the positives and the negatives but nothing that resembled my original list which I had written and then discarded. The negative was the stick I got from a lot of men in the audience. The positive was the number of young ladies who thought they could straighten me out by their irresistible charms. It would have been very rude of me not to let them try (wink wink).

The Mossblown Plaque

I had been elected as the Wrestlers' Reunion Scotland's Honorary President for a couple of years and had learned of the Mossblown

Gym. This establishment was responsible for turning out many good and even great wrestlers from Scotland and was started by the organiser of the present-day reunion. I soon discovered that, although closed many years ago, it was fondly remembered by all who trained there. In my early wrestling years, I remember visiting it on one of my trips to Scotland, though the actual details escape me. As I lived down in Hampshire, my input into the reunion was limited to say the least and usually confined to the actual weekend of the reunion. I always felt that I wasn't able to pull my weight as it was, that year, that Andrew Bryden, who had wrestled in the day as Dale Storm, took me to where the old Mossblown Gym had been situated, although it had been demolished many years ago and today had been replaced with the local library, a lovely building – it was just a shame that the gym had to go but that is progress. I felt quite sad about it, as a lot of history had been sacrificed along the way.

This played on my mind for the rest of that weekend and by the time I had arrived back home on the Tuesday, I had made my mind up that I was going to try to do something about it.

After a bit of thought, I concluded that it would be fitting if they could erect some sort of plaque within the library to remember this once well used and well loved gym.

I contacted Andrew that day and suggested my idea to him. Luckily, he thought the same as me and so it was that I decided to go for it. I immediately sent an email to the Ayrshire County Council, outlining my wishes and could they please assist me in my quest. It took a couple of weeks, but I finally had a reply from Human Resources informing me that they would be redirecting my request to the correct department and that I should hear from them shortly.

It took a couple of weeks, but I finally got a very pleasant email from the Arts, Museums and Libraries department. A very polite person by the name of Gerry informed me that they thought it was a super idea and would see to it that, subject to the boss's approval something would be done along the lines I had suggested.

That's it, I thought, we've done it. I should have known that it was never going to be that simple, as there were certain hoops that had to be jumped through before we hit the winning post. The first was to attend a site meeting that had been suggested for the following week. I politely wrote back that as I lived hundreds of miles away in Hampshire, would they mind if I sent a representative along who would inform me of any information resulting from the meeting. That wish was granted, and I decided to contact Andrew Bryden, who agreed to attend in my absence. He contacted me after the meeting and informed me that Gerry was not as I had imagined him to be, a large Scotsman with a big ginger beard who sounded like Brian Blessed, but a petite lady who was very excited at the whole prospect of bringing this enterprise to a satisfactory conclusion.

There were a few more hoops to negotiate such as size and type of plaque, location of said plaque and various other bits and pieces that needed attention. The date was set for the grand unveiling, which we negotiated to be the day before the reunion. It was attended on the day by the staff of the library, a local MP, Council Members, local press and quite a few of the members of the old Mossblown Gym. The plaque was unveiled by Lillian Bryden, the first lady of Scottish wrestling, who I believe used to wrestle as Diamond Lil. Speeches were made, with bubbly to toast the occasion, accompanied by nibbles, lots of photographs, interviews and lots of handshakes for a job well done.

Members and friends of the old Mossblown Gym

Sanjay The Promoter

Sanjay Bagga is a modern-day promoter who puts his shows on up and down the country nearly every day of the week, sometimes two shows in different venues in the same day. He is one of those wrestling heroes who has not only brought many young up-and-coming wrestlers into the business but has kept the game going when a lot of people had given up with wrestling and consigned it to that historical scrap heap.

Yes, it has changed a bit since my day but that is what the audience want to see. We were lucky, we only had four channels on the television to compete with, and we also had wrestling on ITV, which was our shop window, showing on a Saturday afternoon and for a while, one night during the week. That was until Greg Dyke decided to take it off air in 1986. Was it taken off too soon? In my opinion, yes it was. There are many theories as to why it was removed but I think it was a financial decision, something to do with the advertising industry. However, we shall never know. The introduction of WWE wrestling brought it back to our screens much later with a new image and a new format that re-captured the audiences of today.

Sanjay and his LDN Promotions is one of many that have brought wrestling back to the community in a big way, even though there is more competition than we had in our day. More television channels, any films you want on tap at the touch of a button, better effects have been introduced for programmes. There are games to play from all over the world, all designed to keep the younger people glued to their screens. Competition from all quarters, and yet people still make their ways to the local halls to see the live entertainment that only wrestling can supply.

So let us all raise a glass and celebrate Sanjay and all the others like him for not only providing us with entertainment in the square ring again but for preventing wrestling from going the way of the dinosaurs.

In Your Dreams

It was at the reunion in Blackpool, a few years ago, that a wrestler flew in from America to attend. This was not a rare occasion as most years we would get wrestlers from Sweden, Spain and Germany, to name but three.

I'm not going to give his name, but many wrestlers will know him and those at the reunion will remember the outcome. He seemed to be an okay sort of guy and would join in with the general wrestling talk, telling us how wrestling was conducted over the pond and how he frequented the reunions over there. He even mentioned the Cauliflower Alley Club, the most well-known, prestigious and indeed the largest in the world. Of course, he was a member.

We listened to his tales, we listened and listened, and listened again, on and on he went all weekend. People he knew, people he had fought, people he had beat, on and on and on.

We all went out for a pub meal the evening before the reunion, and he came too. Having our fill of food and a fair bit of libation, I pitched in and asked him to tell us about his career. Big mistake, on and on he went, so I took the easy way out and said I was going out for a cigarette.

One by one, all the other wrestlers came out to join me and boy did I get it in the neck from all of them. 'What did you want to ask him that for?' came at me from all quarters (that was just the clean one. There were many more that can't be printed).

The next morning however, there was a surprise in store. One of our troupe was something of an authority on wrestling over the centuries and this included having a couple of contacts over the water in the Cauliflower Alley Club. The upshot of it was she had found out that our Mr American had never been a wrestler, was not and had never been a member of any wrestling fraternity, in fact had no wrestling skills to his name.

He was confronted with this evidence but insisted that this was untrue, and he would prove it with photos of his time in the ring. Until he could do so, he avoided the rest of us by standing outside of the hotel for hours on end or taking to his room. I don't think he even appeared on the day of the reunion. After the weekend I heard that he had sent several pictures of what he said was himself in the ring. Every one of them was wrestlers that our sharp-eyed historian could give a name to and none of them were pictures of him. He had been found out.

He was never seen at another reunion but there was talk that he now attends a reunion in France. The sad part of it was that if he had come along and said he wasn't a wrestler but a fan, he would have been made most welcome, many fans were and always will be.

A Quick Catch Up

For those of you that have kindly read my last book, there were a few stories about my earlier escapades in the ring that I can now bring up to date.

You may well remember the one where we were wrestling in Wales and had a contingent from the building next door to say that they were paranormal investigators trying to do their stuff next door but as we were making so much noise they couldn't concentrate. The promoter calmed them down and promised that if they wanted to watch the wrestling for the last hour, he would send around a couple of wrestlers to take part in their investigations. Yes, I was one of the ones who was made to volunteer if wanted to work for him in the future.

I won't bore you with the details, but I finished my story with a wish that I would like to get more interested in paranormal investigation at some time in the future when I had the time. Many years later when I joined such a group based in Gloucester. By then, I had moved to Hampshire, so it was a bit of a drive every time, but it turned out to be well worth becoming a member of GAPS, Gloucester Active Paranormal Society, run by the ghost lady of Gloucester, Lyn Cinderey. I stayed with them for many years with varying results.

Several years later I heard from Lyn Cindery again, asking me if I had ever come across a wrestler who wrestled by the name of Ken Banks. You could have knocked me down with a feather. Ken was my mate when I very first started wrestling and we spent quite a while fighting at the local fairgrounds in my early days. Those who have read my first book will know that we spent weeks together making up a travelling wrestling ring from an old boxing ring in his back garden.

'How do you know him, Lyn?' I asked.

'Oh he's a good mate of my brother-in-law.' I couldn't believe it; I had been trying to track him down for many years with no luck and here he was falling into my lap. She furnished me with his telephone number and that night we chatted on the phone for hours.

'When did you stop wrestling?' I enquired.

'About the same time that you left off working for Associated Promotions.' That must have been the early to mid 70s, I thought.

'What did you do then?' I enquired.

'I went on to play in a group, a tribute group of the Shadows. I took the part of Hank Marvin. It turned out to be better than wrestling, more money, home every night and you didn't get hurt.' He did make me laugh, although I remember he was a very good guitarist and had been in various groups in the years previously. We keep in touch by phone, and I have visited him at his home and will again in the not-too-distant future.

Proper Celebrities

Is it just me, or don't we have proper celebrities anymore? There was a time when a celebrity was a well-known television performer. Now you can become one by sitting at home and being filmed watching the telly.

We had celebrities in the wrestling game. The ones that come to mind were the well-known show jumper Harvey Smith, and of course, that bloke whose name I won't mention who had long white hair and smoked cigars. But the real celebrity wrestlers made such an impression that they were persuaded to take part in pantomimes as well as a few who appeared in television programmes such as Les Dawson's sketches, The Generation Game and Bullseye, to name but a few. Many went on to appear in many films and adverts, while a few went on to make a career out of acting. Pat Roach, who was probably best known as Bomber Bussbridge in Auf Wiedersehen Pet and the James Bond films, Raiders of the Lost Ark and many more besides.

Then there was Brian Glover, who wrestled as Leon Arras but then went into acting under his own name. I stand to be corrected but

I think that his first role was in the film Kes, where he played the PE teacher. He went on to work in Porridge and then played a villain in The Sweeney and much more besides. He was also a well-thought-of Shakespearian actor taking on many of the well-known parts, as well as parts in costume dramas. Another one that comes to mind was Paul Luty. I'm sure there are others who have done exceedingly well in the world of entertainment, having started their working lives in the ring.

That's The Spirit

If you read my first book, you may remember the time when, with another wrestler, I found myself spending a night in a haunted house. I hinted that I found the whole experience fascinating and would like, at some time in the future to look further into the world of ghost hunting.

It was many years later having hung up my boots and gave up dragging by backside around the U.K. when I contacted 'The Ghost Lady of Gloucester' also known as Lyn Cinderey, who runs several ghost hunts in and around that area, or to give it the proper title, Paranormal Investigations.

My first haunted building was the well-known Woodchester Mansion near Stroud. A part renovated and part derelict place owned by the National Trust. It was such an interesting place that I was lucky enough to visit a further eight times.

The activity was so intense and every time I entered the kitchen area; I would end up having my face and hand scratched so that they would bleed. It was then that I would become a guinea pig for the whole group as they did their many tests on what could only be described as a phenomenon. One such test was for my hands and face to be checked out by many people before entering, a pair of thick welding gloves were placed on my hands (to show that I could not possibly be scratching myself either purposely or accidentally). There was a person on either side of me, holding my arms out and making sure that my hands stayed inside the gloves. It would still happen on all occasions that the scratches still came, even under the gloved hand. The boffins that be, pondered all this activity and the consensus was that it was caused by a spirit cat who had taken offence to the hearing aid in my right ear, maybe it could hear some sort of high pitch noise that we could not. One last point worth mentioning was that If I was near a wall my face would be targeted but if I were in the centre of the room, it would be my hand. (Sounds like there would have been shelves around the walls.) The other fact was that these scratches would disappear within a few hours with no scab formation or any mark at all. No one can guarantee that it was paranormal activity but if it wasn't then what was it. I leave you to make up your own mind.

Glitterboy Goes Wild

I had been in practice for several years in my second chosen career and I guess it would have been around November 2011 when a regular patient of mine strode into my surgery one morning. She had brought an American friend with her and asked if, after I had treated her, I would mind looking at her friend's back as she had been in pain for several months. This I was happy to do and once my examination was completed, I told her that it would take several treatments, but it could be greatly improved.

She informed me that she would be leaving the country in the morning so I told her that the next time that she was over here, perhaps she would allow me to help her with her back problem. This was most agreeable to her, and so it was left.

A couple of weeks later I next saw my regular patient and having treated her, she asked me if I did home visits. I stated that was so because some patients were too incapacitated to even get out of bed or could not travel for some reason therefore, I would visit them in their homes. Her next question knocked me for six, how would I fancy doing a home visit to Kenya? 'Kenya, you mean the one in East. Africa?' 'Yes, that one' she replied.

After a few stutters and stammers, I replied that I would need to talk it over with my wife and would call her in the morning with my answer. My wife agreed that it would be a good thing to make the trip and that I might regret it if I didn't take the opportunity which had presented itself. It's not often that you get offered an all-expenses trip for a couple of weeks to somewhere where the sun was always shining. My telephone call of acceptance was made early next morning, and my trip was scheduled for mid-February. Within a few weeks, I had sorted out my visa, obtained some American dollars and Kenyan shillings, made a packing list and booked a taxi to Heathrow and back. Christmas and New Year had passed, and my departure date soon arrived. It wasn't long before I was sitting in the taxi early on a February morning on my way to Nairobi and wondering what the hell I was doing undertaking this at my age.

After a long and boring nine-and-a-half-hour flight I finally arrived in this strange place and wondered if there would be a friendly face waiting for me outside Arrivals. I needn't have worried as I saw a young African boy holding up a placard with my name on it. He introduced himself as Peter and told me that he was my driver for the next couple of weeks. I need to tell you at this stage that the lady I was going to see was in fact not living in America as I had assumed all those months ago but was in fact the wife of some rather high-up member of the staff of the American Embassy to Kenya, so I would be staying in the Embassy compound.

During the journey of about 55 minutes I chatted freely with my chauffeur, who, to my relief, spoke perfect English. He filled me in on what to do and indeed, what not to do whilst I was a guest in that country and what Kenyan life was all about. Some details were very enlightening and others bloody frightening.

Eventually we arrived at our destination, where I was to renew the acquaintance of my patient and meet her husband and two children. I was supplied with a few welcome cups of tea and some light supper and given a quick tour of where I would be staying. Then, with apologies, I took to my bed. I had been travelling for hours, and I was totally exhausted.

The following day, after a hearty breakfast, I was introduced to the young girl who would be providing me with my meals, washing, cleaning etc, and then it was time for the first treatment of the day. That taken care of, the rest of my morning was my own. I spent it sitting in the garden, in a nice, shaded spot, reading my Kindle. If I remember correctly, it was the works of Sherlock Holmes, a particular favourite of mine.

The young girl came over and asked if wanted a drink. 'A cup of tea would be nice, thank you' I replied and told her that I drink a lot of tea. She took me at my word and brought me out a fresh cup every twenty minutes. Eventually I had to ask her if she could make it every hour as even I couldn't manage that amount, and I was getting waterlogged. I must admit I was being spoiled rotten and enjoying every minute of it.

Eventually, it was time for the second treatment. That completed, I enjoyed a nice lunch and then it was time to seek out the pool, which was situated a few minutes away. It was a lovely pool, and I spent the afternoon between swimming and reading. I almost had the pool to myself apart from the odd mother and toddler, who informed me that the pool didn't get busy until about 5.30pm when people finished work.

I left the pool area and sauntered back to my rooms, changed into my clothes and administered the third and final treatment of the day, before my evening meal. After that, it was back out on to the veranda to read, relax and watch the twinkling lights of Nairobi in the distance. I retired to my bed about 11 pm to get a good night's sleep before the morning, when I would do it all again. It was a hard life I had here, but someone had to do it.

This went on for another few days and without sounding ungrateful, I was beginning to get a bit bored. However, I was told that as tomorrow was Saturday, I was to be taken on a couple of trips to see some of the local sanctuaries. First was the world-famous Daphne Sheldrick elephant sanctuary, where young elephants who had been found orphaned were taken to look after them until they reached adulthood and could be released into the wild again. A very interesting place to visit if ever you get the chance. Then we travelled over a very busy road to the giraffe sanctuary, where I stood on a platform and fed the giraffes. The following day I was taken into the Nairobi National Park to do a day's game drive. Now that was a day to remember. Situated on the edge of Nairobi, it extends for miles. It was home to many of Africa's wild animals and we saw many different species during the day. My guide was very knowledgeable about all the different animals that we came across.

It was getting dark when we left the park and I was told that if I wanted to come back in the morning, I could stroke a tame cheetah. Now there's an offer you don't get given very often back home.

It was then that I made a big mistake. I phoned my wife and told her I would be stroking a tame cheetah. Now my dear wife had two ambitions in life: one was to go on safari and the other was to see a cheetah in the wild. She always watches the wildlife programmes on the television and her favourite ones were filmed in the Massai Mara. I could tell by the tone of her voice that she was turning into the green-eyed monster and the only way I was ever going to pacify her was to promise her a safari the following year, and what's more I knew that she wasn't going to let me forget it.

As it turned out, I never got to stroke the cheetah. My driver was clearly under instruction not to let me get into any danger at all, and he informed me that like a tame domestic cat, when you stopped stroking, it would sometimes lift its paw and give you a little scratch. The cheetah doesn't retract its claws, so it might just open your stomach. Knowing the standard of health and safety, I declined the offer.

The following few days went as expected and my patient was really on the mend. My tan was getting darker, and my swimming was improving no end.

It was soon Saturday once again and I was taken on a long trip to a place called Nakuru, which is near a huge lake in the rift valley. A beautiful part of Kenya indeed, where we would be staying for the weekend in a type of lodge. A great adventure, but I was warned that we needed to keep a look out for lions, leopards and worst of all hippos. The hippos come out of the water after sundown and wander around feeding. They are bad-tempered and kill more people every year than all the other predators put together. Oh, and just mind that you don't step on a snake because you will probably die. Other than that, have a wonderful weekend.

At about ten o clock at night, mine host insisted that we go and sit on the veranda with a gin and tonic to see if we could see some hippos. Luckily, we gave up just after midnight and I was never happier than when I crawled into bed that night. Next day we visited the lake and saw about a million flamingos all around the lake and about 50 yards deep. It was a sight to see, like a big pink bow tied around the whole lake but, my lord, did they stink. Apparently, they lay their eggs on piles of their droppings to keep them out of the water.

In the afternoon we visited another game park named Hell's Gate, in a huge valley with high rocks all around. It was formed many moons ago when the rift valley formed from a huge earthquake.

Eventually it was time for the long journey back to Nairobi, as I was returning to England early the next morning. My patient was better, and my work was done. Thank you, Kenya, it has been a blast.

We did return the following year on our first proper safari. My wife didn't forget and what I didn't allow for was that my good lady insisted on having the correct safari clothes etc to go with, and of course a new state of the art camera with a choice of lenses, not forgetting a proper pair of binoculars. It had cost us a fortune and we hadn't even got our arses on the plane yet.

We were fortunate enough to book with a company which had been experienced in the safari business for many years, so it was all organised for the following August. With the memory of my previous trip still firmly in my mind and the thought of such a long flight time, I decided that we would fly first class. Bugger it, if we couldn't do it at our time of life, then when could we? We would be starting off staying a night in a posh hotel in Nairobi, then visiting a place called Samburu for a couple of days, then into the Aberdare mountains and on to the Masai Mara and finally a last day in Naivasha and back to Nairobi. It sounded great, which of course it was. We arrived at Samburu late afternoon after a six-hour drive and were greeted by the camp staff ready with an ice-cold drink and a nice damp cool towel to freshen our faces.

My wife took one look out of the camp and into the wild flat plain and saw a lonely bull elephant standing under the only tree in view. She did what she does when she is overcome with emotion and burst into tears. The camp staff were rather concerned until I explained that they had done nothing wrong, and it was her usual reaction to such a beautiful setting. After that, they referred to her as 'the lady that cries tears of joy'.

It was later that evening when we asked if we would see cheetahs in Samburu. They told us that they had not seen them there for a few years but assured us that we would see them when we got to the Masai Mara. We were up at 4 am the next day to go on our first game drive. We had been out for about twenty minutes and just as the daylight was breaking through, we suddenly stopped. I looked out of the window and about ten yards ahead, I saw it. 'Look, it's a bloody cheetah!' My wife leapt out of her seat with such speed to see out of my window, that she hit my head with her ample bosom, pushing me so hard that my head bounced off the glass. She managed to get some good photos. Finally her dream had come true.

When we arrived in the Mara, we were not disappointed and were treated to many great game drives with sightings of not only the big five (cape buffalo, lions, leopards, elephants and rhinos) but many other delights that Africa had to offer. A highlight of the whole trip was a hot-air balloon ride early in the morning over the plains of the Masai Mara with a champagne breakfast once we had landed. To conclude, it was indeed the holiday of a lifetime, so much so that we went on safari again and again, year after year, and hope to do so again soon. By the time we visited last, we were what you might call seasoned travellers in that life.

We had started off by going on a well-organised trip of about thirty people and staying in camps with high chain link fences all around, travelling by road for about six hours between places, but it was all great fun. On the last one we flew in small airplanes between camps, landing in some airstrips laid out in a clearing in the bush and staying in luxury tents, in camps with no fence around it and run entirely by the Masai people. Many times we woke up early in the morning to the rasping sounds of lions licking dew off the tent canvas. In the way of the safari set, we had arrived. Happy days.

Ian 'Teddy Bear' Taylor

I have met many people in the wrestling game over the years. Some have been just nodding acquaintances, some colleagues, many have become friends and quite a few have become good friends, while a few have become great friends and good buddies. Ian 'Teddy bear' Taylor is certainly among the last category. All through our wrestling careers we never actually met, although we must have seen each other as during my younger days, I had visited the Mossblown Gym in Ayr Scotland which was Ian's training ground. It was at the Blackpool reunion that we introduced ourselves and from then, our friendship flourished. We had much to talk about and have got to know each other well over the years.

During one of these interesting conversations he told me that he had done a couple of programmes on Ayrshire Online Radio, one of them being a daily show and the other a weekly Country and Western show. Country and Western has been one of my favourite brands of music for many years and so I listened in. What an absolute joy it was and from then on, I rarely missed a show. I did eventually, with Ian's permission, do a small music quiz for this show every week which ran for quite a while, and I found it very enjoyable.

Every year whilst attending the Wrestlers' Reunion Scotland, I would travel up a day early, Ian would pick me up from the station and drive me to my hotel, then we would meet up that evening and have a meal together. Over the years, it has become a great ritual and one I really look forward to. He has been good enough to run me here and there and has even taken me on a tour around the place to see the sights and history of the local area, which is always appreciated. At the Blackpool reunion, we always make time to go out for a couple of meals and a good old natter. We speak often throughout the year, thanks to the internet and the telephone. A great friend indeed and what's more, a great friend for life.

Billy La Rue

This Kent-based wrestler went on to become one of the UK's great ambassadors for the sport, travelling internationally to ply his trade. We are of course talking about the middleweight star Billy La Rue. Although Billy had a great love for boxing it was Basil Riley, who himself was already involved in the industry, who persuaded him to pursue a career in professional wrestling. The two became firm friends and after training at Frank Prices gym Billy had his first professional bout in 1968. Initially he started working for independent promoters throughout the south of the country, but he soon came to the attention of the hierarchy at Dale Martin promotions and made the move to join their ranks. Due to the vast number of shows Dales were promoting in those days, work was plenty, and he found himself wrestling most nights of the week.

International success soon followed, and he found himself travelling to Germany, Spain and other European countries. He continued to do this for a number of years dividing himself between the UK and Europe.

When Billy retired from the ring, he kept in contact with his former colleagues. He was a regular attendee at the Bridge's reunion in Kent for many years and one of the participants at some of the legends shows promoted by LDN Wrestling.

In 2023, he was one of the invited guests at the Annual Wrestling Lunch in Watford and was presented with an award in 2024. Billy La Rue is without any doubt is one of the nicest men in the industry today. His in-ring ability speaks for itself and he more than deserves any accolades that come his way for his years of commitment to the wrestling business.

I have had the good fortune to meet up with Billy at several of the reunions. I remember that it only took the first meeting for us to become friends, and it was a pleasure to chat with him and his lovely wife Catherine. A few years ago, they both visited me at my home, which resulted in a nostalgic trip down memory lane whilst munching our way through one of my wife's home-made cakes.

Whenever we meet up now we take the rise out of each other, all in good humour. They are a lovely couple and as I have said before, both great ambassadors for the world of wrestling.

Wrestling Heritage

For those of you who would like to know more about the golden years of wrestling there are several avenues open to you, on the Internet, Facebook etc as well as in book form. It is even available on Amazon Kindle. For my own preference, you couldn't do better than to join the Heritage Website.

The site was launched on 13th April 2007 by two wrestling enthusiasts/historians by the names of Anglo Italian and Alan 'Hack' Bamber. These two got to know each other on a wrestling forum held in 2004, although it was a further two years before they met in person when Anglo came to England on business from Italy. It was on this meeting that they planned the Heritage site, and since then they have met up either in the UK or in Italy. Hack had watched wrestling from the age of 11 years whilst living in Lancashire and Anglo, who at that time was living in Hastings, has a Dale Martin background.

The weekly newsletter has a circulation of 280, there are 1908 different wrestlers in the A-to-Z section, listed under 2,384 different names, and there are 1,267 web pages on the site. As well as the

website, they often help journalists, authors and family members to research wrestlers and wrestling history. The daily average of visitors to the site is between 500 to 700. In 2012 following the televising of the wrestling documentary called
'Time Shift' the site hit over 10,000 visitors on a single day, probably due to both Anglo and Alan making an appearance on this documentary.

I have had the pleasure in meeting up with Alan (Hack) at many reunions over the recent years and we have become good friends. I have been his opposite number as comperes during the award presentations at the Wrestlers' Reunions Scotland. We are also in touch frequently.

Some Kind Words About My Last Book

I recently read your book *Confessions of a Wrestler* and it was brilliant. I liked the way you covered the history of how you got started in wrestling and it showed how much work you had to put into it, especially the amount of travelling to the venues and how you had to arrive on time.

Also, I liked the adventures you shared and the scrapes that you got into with your wrestling colleagues. They did make me laugh. I also liked the wrestlers that you met and shoulders with and looked up to as your heroes when you were younger. I was a great fan of the Saturday afternoon wrestling on the television back in the day, people like Mark Rocco, Marty Jones, Fit Finlay, Adrian Street, Bobby Barnes to name but a few. I used to go to Fairfield Halls, Croydon, with my Nan. Sending you this has brought back many memories.

Once again, thank you for writing this book and sharing your career, it was a brilliant insight into wrestling and a great book to read. My favourite was when you were wrestling and there was a power cut, I wish I could have been there to see the faces on the audience when the lights came back on, and they realized what had been going on.
- Andrew Pickersgill.

5 out of 5 stars. An enjoyable read, Confessions of a Wrestler, from the wrestler himself.

I thoroughly enjoyed reading this book, an amazing journey in the life of a Professional British wrestler in the days when wrestling was wrestling. I couldn't put the book down when I started reading and by the time I had finished, Martin had taken me back to when wrestling was a family show, and I wouldn't have missed those Saturday afternoons (thank you for that). He speaks of his journey and gives a very dignified prospective of his own personal experience and that is what made the book so enjoyable for me. Telling it as you had lived it.

I would highly recommend this book to any wrestling enthusiast because in my own opinion, it's amazing throughout. Thanks Martin.
- Thomas Wright

The Mattress

It was a couple of years ago when I decided that it was time to take an old mattress to the local dump. My wife had been on about it for a while, I don't know why, I said I would do it and there was no need for her to remind me every six months. It was only a single one, so I knew that if I rolled it up length ways, it would go into the car with the back seats down. Having found a ball of old string in the shed, I struggled to tie it up. That was one bout that I finally won, but it was touch and go a couple of times. With a bit of grunt and groan, I managed to force it into the car and there was room on the front seat for an old coffee table that we no longer needed. I stood it up and put the seat belt around it, safety first I thought.

Off I set for the ten-mile trip, down the A303 to the dump. After about ten minutes, there was an almighty crack. The bloody string had broken and in a split second, the car was full of mattress. There I was, driving along one of the busiest roads in the area, with my nose about six inches from the windscreen and a mattress bouncing on and off my head with a regular beat, like Staying Alive by the Bee Gees.

After a nightmare trip I arrived at the dump and pulled into the unloading bay. Managing to get out of the car without the mattress spewing out after me, I started to open the boot when a bloke in a high-viz jacket shouted at me. 'You can't drive in, you have to reverse.'

'If I do that, then I won't be able to get the mattress out of the car,' I replied. He came over and looked in the car. 'I can't help that; those are the rules' he said pushing his chest out over his beer belly. I reversed the car into the space and asked him if he could possibly give me a hand with the mattress. 'No, more than my job's worth' he said, shaking his head, 'health and safety.' 'Whose health and safety?' I asked in a sarcastic tone. 'Mine of course' and he walked away.

After a fifteen-minute struggle, I managed to get it out of the car and into the skip. It wasn't easy for a pensioner. Now for the coffee table. I undid the safety belt and lifted it out onto the concrete next to the car and as I turned around, there was my jobsworth again. 'Let me take that for you,' he said

I knew full well that he intended to keep it to one side so that he could sell it for a fiver or so. I looked him straight in the eye, lifted my foot and brought it down hard in the centre of the table, smashing it into several pieces. The look on his face was a picture. 'No, it's okay, I'll put it in the skip myself, I don't want you to get a splinter, health and safety you know.' I don't remember how much I had paid for it or how much it cost second hand, but it was worth every penny.

The Flower Show

It was in the late 80s; I was sitting at the table eating a late Sunday breakfast. My wrestling career had come to an end a few years previous. There was a sharp knock at the door and a minute later, my wife ushered in an elderly gentleman. He introduced himself as Colonel Blessington (name changed) from the manor house a few villages away. I waved him to a chair and asked how I could help him, He coughed a couple of times to clear his throat, then began with a voice of cut glass. 'I am the Chairman of the local flower show held in our village, a thankless task but someone has to do it, don't you know.'

'And where do I come into it?' I asked.

He squared his shoulders and began, 'We are short of a celebrity judge and wondered if you could see your way clear to step in, as it were. The usual chap has retired so the committee elected me to find a replacement. Your name was given to me at a dinner party last week.'

I was puzzled. 'Well, I don't know that I'm a celebrity, I certainly wouldn't claim to be.' He stared at me for a moment. 'Weren't you a boxer or something? Judo, maybe a judo champ.'

I frowned at him. 'Well, I used to be a professional wrestler until a few years ago, but if you are looking for a celebrity, then I'm afraid that you are scraping the bottom of the barrel with me.' The whole situation was beginning to amuse me. He began furnishing me with a few details, such as date, time and list of categories for the prizes. Also, the name, address and telephone number of the chap who was to be the other judge. He was a professional gardener by trade and had worked for the local council in the parks and leisure department. He was awaiting my call, assuming that I agreed to do it, there was a meeting of the show committee in three weeks at the village hall, 8 pm, and we would both be required to attend. I agreed to think it over and let him know in a day or two. After lunch on that same day, I rang the other would-be judge and we agreed to meet up in our local pub and talk things over and at 7 pm that evening, we met and introduced ourselves. Simon seemed to be a down to earth sort of chap who, (if you'll pardon the pun,) called a spade a spade. I could see that we were going to get along.

Simon's first impression of the Colonel was the same as mine. 'If the rest of the Committee are the same as him, I think we might be in for a bumpy ride. He thinks that I'm a professional gardener, but Percy Thrower, I am not. I spend my time in summer watering bloody hanging baskets and my winter's, throwing cow sh*t onto flower beds. If he thinks that qualifies me to judge a flower show, then he has been misinformed.'

'I know what you mean, he thinks I'm a Celebrity. Let's agree to do it, it might be a laugh.'

So that was how two nobodies came to judge a flower show. A few weeks later, Simon picked me up in his van and off we went to a committee meeting. 'Just let it go over your head,' he said with a knowing wink. 'I have managed to find out a few things about this committee, it doesn't matter what the subject is, they seem to be the same committee members for everything. Fete, flower show, bowls club, cricket club, I think they must elect each other.' 'I was beginning to think so myself' I replied.

The meeting came and went, and we were invited to say hardly anything, just sit and listen, that seemed to be our role in the proceedings. We would be expected to start early on the Saturday morning to judge the best kept garden award, in and around the village, then have lunch in the pub while we sorted out the winner, which would be Lady Musselwhite as she always wins it, even though she has a full-time gardener. Then, after lunch, we would walk over to the playing field, where we would judge the displays. We were given a list of the people who usually won those categories and told in no uncertain terms that those were the ones to consider. We were glad when the meeting was over, and Simon and I headed for the pub. 'If they think we're going to play their silly games and cheat in order that their cronies get to win, they've got another think coming,' he said. 'My sentiments exactly' I replied. 'We are the judges, so we will judge.'

And we did. The day of the show came around quickly and our judging of the best kept garden had been completed, and wouldn't you know it, the winner wasn't on our list. Oh dear, how sad never mind. Our meal at the pub, which was paid for by the committee funds, went down a treat. I whispered to Simon, 'make the most of it, this is never going to happen again.' I thought he was going to choke on his rib-eye steak.

When the time came, we walked over to the playing fields, where we were shown into the exhibit tent, then left to our own devices. I must admit that although I knew very little about growing flowers, fruit or vegetables, I was impressed by the exhibits. I don't remember anything as grand on my dad's allotment. We did our duty as we saw it, and awarded first, second and third prizes where we saw fit.

One thing we thought surprising was that every exhibit had the owner's name printed neatly by the side, so we knew who had entered what. We thought that was unfair. In our opinion, to make it fair, they should have all been anonymous, but it was quite obvious why they had brought in that rule, how dare they? It must have been pure coincidence that none of the winners were on our list.

I said to Simon, 'are we going to hang around for the prize giving?'

'Are you joking, I wouldn't miss it for a gold watch' he sniggered. We were asked if we would announce the winners, then the Colonel would hand out the rosettes. 'With pleasure,' we said. As we made our way up to the podium, we agreed that we would announce them alternately.

I have been racking my brain to describe the look on the Committee's faces when we announced the prizewinners. Suffice to say, the crowd loved it, but the Committee members were fuming. As the last winners left the podium, we looked at each other and, in unison, said, 'beer tent', and off we went for a well-earned beer or two. 'I don't suppose the beers will be on the Committee, will they' said Simon. 'Perhaps not' I said.

About ten minutes later, the Colonel came over. 'Could I have a word?' he said, in a stern voice. 'What the hell were you playing at, can't you follow simple instructions?'

'Not when it includes defrauding the public,' I said in hot temper. He stammered his reply. 'Nothing to do with defrauding anybody, it's to do with the standing and respect in the community, I don't expect you to understand it.'

Simon pitched in, 'Respect? You don't deserve respect, what you asked us to do was downright disgraceful and what the local newspaper will make of it when we give them our full account of anyone ever again.'

The Colonel turned red with anger, 'you cannot back up your accusations on any of this, so don't come the old soldier with me, my man.'

'Oh no?' said Simon. He held up the list he had given us. 'I believe, Colonel, that this is your handwriting, is it not? on council letterheaded paper?'

I thought the Colonel was going to blow a gasket. He squared his shoulders, turned around and strode off.

We were never intending to inform the local paper, and nothing more was heard from the flower show committee. We were never again asked to judge anything else in that village. However, Simon and I often meet up in the pub for a beer now and then and spend time laughing at our adventure. That will teach them for messing with a local celebrity that no one has ever heard of, or a professional gardener who watered plants and shovelled sh*t for a living.

And Finally...

I would have found it impossible to write this book without the help of some of my family and friends. Those who helped me when I was out of my depth, those who nudged my memory and added those memories that I had forgotten. Not to mention those who encouraged me to write it, so here goes.

To my wife Ruth, who put up with a lot as I talked incessantly about my memories and stepped in when my laptop got the better of me. She also helped me through the publishing maze.

My daughter Chloe, who tried, sometimes in vain, to teach me things on the laptop that I never knew existed and did the superb cover artwork for this book.

To my friend and wrestling superstar Johnny Kincaid, for providing the foreword.

Also to my good mate Ian Taylor for his encouragement throughout.

To the many wrestlers who gave me permission to add their esteemed careers to this book, too many to mention by name. I would also pay my respects to those wrestling friends who have sadly gone to that big dressing room in the sky. And of course, to all those wrestling fans who supported us all of them years ago. without their support we would never have been able to do that which we all loved.

Thank you all.

Printed in Great Britain
by Amazon